The Moral Compass

28 Principles for Integrity-Driven Leadership

By

Moe Rock and Featured Commentary

LA Tribune Publishing

Los Angeles, California

The Right of LA Tribune/Moe Rock to be identified as
the creator and owner of the work has been asserted by them in accordance
with the Copyright Act 1988.

LA TRIBUNE PUBLISHING

name has been established by the LA Tribune.

Printed in the United States of America

ISBN- 979-8-8691-8803-8

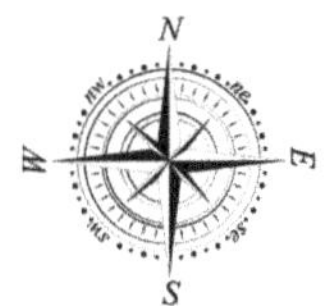

Foreword by Dr. Joe Vitale

Warren Buffett, the CEO of Berkshire Hathaway, once said, "In looking for people to hire, look for three qualities: integrity, intelligence, and energy. And if they don't have the first, the other two will kill you."

Oprah Winfrey, the media mogul, and philanthropist, once said, "Leadership is about empathy. It is about having the ability to relate to and connect with people for the purpose of inspiring and empowering their lives."

That should be enough right there to convince you that integrity and empathy are more than trendy buzzwords; they are essential to the life of your business – and you.

Moreover, that is why this book is so important.

It reveals the 28 principles of integrity and empathy.

In addition, a man who lives what he teaches writes it.

I first met Moe Rock when his company, The Los Angeles Tribune, presented me with their lifetime achievement award. I did not know him at all, but he surprised me by knowing of my life work, including my very early material, such as *The Seven Lost Secrets of Success* and *there is a Customer Born Every Minute.*

We went on to participate in online events. Moe always made a fuss over me, being sure people recognized my contributions to the self-help industry as well as to the world of marketing. I later interviewed him for my e-TV show, Zero Limits Living. I came to know him even better and count him as a new friend.

However, I did not know he was working on an important new book.

He sent me a copy of it. As I reviewed it, I became excited. This is what we need. Far too many in business today are self-obsessed. They need integrity. They need empathy. They need to wake up and discover what really matters in business. This is what can save us all.

You do not have to be a leader in a company to need this information. You are a leader in your family, in your community, in the world at large. Everyone needs to learn the principles of integrity, and here they are.

The 28 principles are unique. You may know one or two of them, but it is unlikely you know all 28. And knowing them is one thing; living them is another. This book will help you do both.

A lifetime of experience went into discovering these laws, and Moe spent months organizing and writing them into a format we can easily digest and use.

This is a practical, inspiring, and life changing book. Read it. Live it. Share it.

Expect Miracles.

Dr. Joe Vitale

Dr. Joe Vitale—once homeless but now a motivating inspirator known to his millions of fans as "Mr. Fire!"—is the world-renowned author of numerous bestselling books, including The Attractor Factor, Zero Limits, The Awakened Millionaire, Karmic Marketing, Hypnotic Writing, The Miracle, and numerous other titles. His online television show "Zero Limits Living" is on over 1,000 platforms. He is considered one of the top 50 most inspiring speakers in the world. He starred in the blockbuster movie The Secret. He has recorded many bestselling audio programs, from The Missing Secret to The Zero Point. He is also a musician with 15 albums. His movie, Zero Limits, will release 2024. His main website is www.MrFire.com

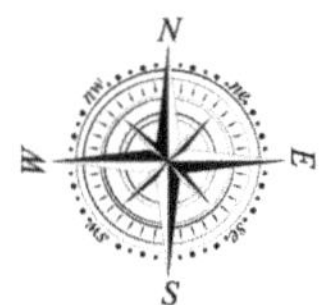

Table of Contents

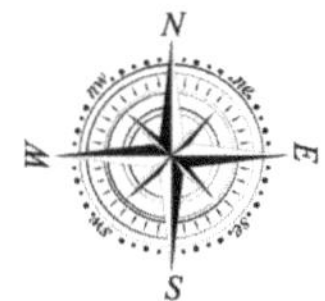

Introduction

Welcome to "The Moral Compass: 28 Principles for Achieving Integrity-Driven Success," a transformative guide to unlocking your potential and becoming the best version of yourself. As you embark on this journey of self-discovery and growth, you will be guided by 28 principles that will revolutionize the way you live, work, and lead.

Throughout history, the world has been shaped by incredible leaders who have inspired and changed the course of humanity. From John F. Kennedy to Oprah Winfrey to Mahatma Gandhi, these leaders have all shared a common trait - a strong moral compass rooted in integrity and compassion. They stood for something greater than themselves, and as a result, they left a profound impact on the world.

This book is your opportunity to learn the leadership skills that were applied by great historical leaders and embrace their principles of integrity-driven success. By doing so, you will gain the tools and insights needed to lead with purpose and make a positive impact on the world around you.

Through proven universal principles, actionable advice, and powerful insights, you will gain a deeper understanding of the significance of integrity in your personal and professional life. You will discover how to cultivate empathy, embrace vulnerability, and communicate effectively, all while staying true to your core values.

This book is not just about achieving personal success, but about making a positive impact on the world around you. It is about living a life of purpose and leaving a lasting legacy of integrity and compassion.

Whether you are a young professional just starting out, a seasoned leader looking to make a change, or anyone in between, this book is for you. By embracing these 28 principles and living with integrity, you will become a powerful force for positive change in the world.

So let us begin this journey together, learning from the examples of the great leaders who came before us and using their principles to guide us towards a brighter, more ethical future. The world needs more leaders like you, leaders who lead with integrity and compassion, and who inspire others to do the same.

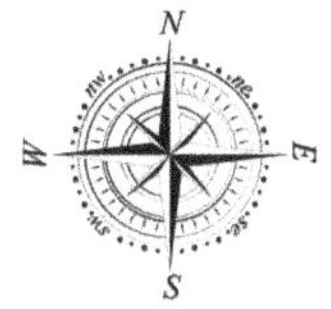

Chapter 1

Moral Compass Principle One: Embracing Integrity: The Cornerstone of Personal Growth

"Integrity is the essence of everything successful."
– Buckminster Fuller

In the vast landscape of personal development, one quality stands out as the foundation for success and fulfillment - integrity. Imagine a world where everyone acted with honesty, respect, and ethical behavior. It may sound like a lofty goal, but it is possible. By embracing integrity as the cornerstone of personal growth, we can make a significant difference not only in our own lives but also in the lives of those around us.

Integrity is not just a buzzword or a vague concept. It is the unwavering commitment to act in accordance with our core values, even when faced with challenging situations or potential personal loss. When we make integrity a central aspect of our lives, we become reliable and trustworthy individuals, both in our personal lives and as leaders. This reliability forms the basis for strong relationships, effective communication, and successful collaboration.

More than just a virtue, embracing integrity is essential for achieving success and fulfillment. It fosters self-respect and self-worth, leading to increased self-awareness and personal growth. By acting in accordance with our core values, we become more conscious of our actions, thoughts, and feelings. Life changing

As leaders, it is crucial to understand that integrity is not just a personal quality. It is also the foundation of effective leadership. When leaders act with integrity, they create a culture of trust and transparency, which leads to increased productivity, employee satisfaction, and organizational success. In contrast, leaders who lack integrity often create a toxic work environment that stifles creativity and undermines morale.

To fully embrace integrity as the cornerstone of personal growth and leadership, it is essential to take actionable steps toward living and leading with integrity. Start by identifying your core values and evaluating your current level of integrity. Then, set integrity-based goals, seek feedback, and practice mindfulness. Learn from role models, hold yourself accountable, develop empathy, and create a culture of integrity.

Throughout history, there have been countless examples of leaders who have embraced integrity as the cornerstone of their personal growth and leadership. One such example is Mahatma Gandhi, who led India to independence through a nonviolent civil disobedience campaign. Gandhi's commitment to integrity was unwavering, and he refused to compromise his principles, even in the face of imprisonment and violence. He stood for something greater than himself, and as a result, he inspired millions of people around the world to embrace nonviolent resistance as a means of achieving social and political change.

Another example is Nelson Mandela, who spent 27 years in prison for his opposition to apartheid in South Africa. Despite the injustices he faced, Mandela never lost sight of his commitment to integrity and forgiveness. He worked tirelessly to dismantle the apartheid system and establish a democratic and inclusive society. Through his leadership, Mandela demonstrated the power of integrity in achieving lasting change and inspiring others to do the same.

How to Apply the Moral Compass:

Identify your core values: Take some time to reflect on your beliefs and values, making a list of those that are most important to you. This will help you better understand your moral compass and guide your decisions and actions in alignment with your principles.

Assess your current level of integrity: Evaluate your recent decisions and actions, identifying areas where you may have compromised your values or acted in a manner inconsistent with your principles. Use this assessment as an opportunity to learn and grow, setting goals for improvement.

Set integrity-based goals: Establish specific, measurable goals related to living and leading with integrity. Develop a plan for achieving these goals and track your progress over time.

Seek feedback: Request honest feedback from trusted friends, family members, or colleagues regarding your integrity. Use this feedback as an opportunity for growth and improvement.

Practice mindfulness: Cultivate mindfulness through meditation, journaling, or other techniques to help you become more self-aware and make intentional, integrity-driven decisions.

Learn from role models: Identify individuals who exemplify integrity in their personal and professional lives. Observe their actions and decisions, seeking to learn from their example.

Hold yourself accountable: When you make a commitment or decision, ensure that you follow through and take responsibility for the outcomes. If you falter in upholding your integrity, acknowledge your mistake, learn from it, and take steps to make amends and prevent it from happening again.

Develop empathy: Strive to understand and appreciate the perspectives and feelings of others. This will help you make more compassionate and fair decisions, further reinforcing your commitment to integrity.

Create a culture of integrity: As a leader, work towards fostering an environment that value and promotes honesty, transparency, and ethical behavior. Encourage open communication and support team members in their efforts to act with integrity.

Celebrate your successes: Recognize and celebrate your achievements and progress in embracing integrity, both in your personal life and as a leader. This will help reinforce the importance of integrity and motivate you to continue your journey toward integrity-driven success.

Remember to celebrate your successes along the way. Recognize and celebrate your achievements and progress in embracing integrity, both in your personal life and as a leader. By implementing these actionable tips and activities, you will be well on your way to embracing integrity as the cornerstone of your personal growth journey. As you continue to develop this essential quality, you will find that you are better equipped to navigate the challenges of life and leadership, achieving lasting success, and making a meaningful impact on the lives of those around you.

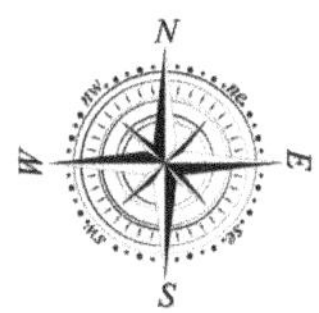

Chapter 2

Cultivating Self-Awareness – The Key to Authentic Leadership

"Who looks outside, dreams; who looks inside, awakes."

– Carl Jung

What separates a great leader from a good one? It is self-awareness - the ability to understand oneself deeply, identify one's strengths and weaknesses, and empathize with others. In other words, self-awareness is the cornerstone of authentic leadership. In this chapter, we will explore the importance of self-awareness, discuss strategies to cultivate it, and provide actionable tips to help you apply it in your leadership journey.

Self-awareness empowers us to make informed decisions, forge deep connections, and lead with integrity. It helps us recognize our emotions, values, and beliefs, and thus, we can manage them better. When we are self-aware, we can understand our impact on others and adjust our behavior accordingly. With self-awareness, we can leverage our strengths, identify areas for improvement, and lead more authentically.

Here are some strategies to develop self-awareness:

Practice mindfulness: Mindfulness allows us to be fully present in the moment and observe our thoughts and emotions non-judgmentally. Engage in practices like meditation, deep breathing, and journaling to develop a deeper understanding of your inner world.

Seek feedback: Feedback from people you trust can provide valuable insights into your leadership style, strengths, and areas of improvement. Be open to receiving feedback and use it to become a better leader.

Reflect on experiences: Regularly reflect on your experiences - both positive and negative - to identify patterns in your behavior, beliefs, and values. This reflection can help you gain deeper insights into your motivations and potential blind spots.

Historical example: Abraham Lincoln's authentic leadership through self-awareness

To further illustrate the importance of self-awareness in leadership, let us examine the case of Abraham Lincoln, the 16th President of the United States. Lincoln is considered one of the greatest leaders in history due to his remarkable ability to navigate the country through the tumultuous times of the Civil War.

Lincoln demonstrated exceptional self-awareness throughout his presidency. He was acutely aware of his strengths and weaknesses and used this understanding to make strategic decisions. For example, recognizing his own limitations, Lincoln assembled a "team of rivals" by appointing political adversaries to his cabinet. This move allowed him to gather diverse perspectives and opinions, fostering a more balanced and effective decision-making process.

Furthermore, Lincoln's self-awareness enabled him to manage his emotions effectively, even under immense pressure. He regularly engaged in self-reflection, writing letters to himself and others to process his thoughts and feelings. This practice helped him gain perspective and maintain a levelheaded approach to the challenges he faced.

Lincoln's empathy and understanding of others were also rooted in his self-awareness. He often put himself in the shoes of others, considering their experiences and viewpoints. This empathetic approach allowed him to connect with people from various backgrounds, fostering unity and collaboration in a deeply divided nation.

In summary, Abraham Lincoln's authentic leadership was grounded in his strong sense of self-awareness. By understanding his own strengths and weaknesses, managing his emotions, and empathizing with others, Lincoln was able to lead the United States through one of its darkest periods. His example serves as a powerful testament to the importance of cultivating self-awareness for effective and authentic leadership.

Here are some actionable tips for applying self-awareness to leadership:

Set aside time for reflection: Schedule regular periods of solitude and introspection to explore your thoughts, feelings, and experiences. Use this time to journal, meditate, or engage in other mindfulness practices that foster self-awareness.

Create a personal mission statement: Develop a clear and concise statement that outlines your core values, passions, and leadership vision. This statement can serve as a guide for your decision-making and help you stay true to your authentic self.

Continuously learn and grow: Embrace a growth mindset and commit to ongoing personal and professional development. By actively seeking new experiences, challenges, and learning opportunities, you will deepen your self-awareness and enhance your leadership abilities.

Practice empathy: Put yourself in the shoes of your team members and colleagues, striving to understand their perspectives and experiences. By demonstrating empathy and compassion, you will foster stronger connections and cultivate a more inclusive and supportive work environment.

In conclusion, cultivating self-awareness is a vital aspect of authentic leadership, enabling us to lead with integrity, empathy, and effectiveness. By applying the strategies and tips outlined in this chapter, you will be well on your way to developing the self-awareness necessary for lasting success and meaningful impact in your personal and professional life. Remember, self-awareness is not a destination; it is a continuous journey of growth, learning, and improvement.

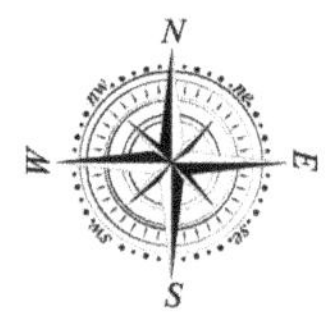

Chapter 3

Developing Empathy Connecting with Others on a Deeper Level

"Each one of us has lived through some devastation, some loneliness, some weather super storm or spiritual super storm, when we look at each other we must say, I understand. I understand how you feel because I have been there myself. We must support each other and empathize with each other because each of us is more alike than we are unalike."

– Maya Angelou

Empathy is a crucial leadership skill that allows us to connect with others on a deeper level, understand their feelings and perspectives, and ultimately foster an inclusive, supportive, and collaborative environment. In this chapter, we will discuss the importance of empathy in leadership, explore strategies for developing empathy, and provide actionable tips for incorporating empathetic leadership into your daily interactions.

The Importance of Empathy in Leadership

Empathy is the ability to understand and share the feelings of others, allowing us to recognize and validate their emotions, concerns, and experiences. In the context of leadership, empathy is essential for building trust, fostering collaboration, and enhancing team performance. By demonstrating empathy, leaders can create an environment in which team members feel valued, respected, and understood, leading to increased engagement, motivation, and commitment.

Strategies for Developing Empathy

Actively listen: One of the most effective ways to cultivate empathy is through active listening, which involves giving your full attention to the speaker, asking open-ended questions, and summarizing their main points to ensure understanding. By practicing active listening, we can better comprehend the emotions, concerns, and perspectives of others, allowing us to respond with empathy and compassion.

Practice perspective taking: Perspective-taking involves putting ourselves in the shoes of others, imagining their thoughts, feelings, and experiences as if they were our own. By regularly engaging in perspective-taking exercises, we can develop a deeper understanding of others and enhance our empathetic abilities.

Cultivate emotional intelligence: Emotional intelligence is the ability to recognize, understand, and manage our emotions, as well as the emotions of others. By developing our emotional intelligence, we can become more attuned to the feelings and needs of those around us, enabling us to respond with empathy and understanding.

Actionable Tips for Incorporating Empathetic Leadership

Prioritize emotional connection: Focus on building emotional connections with your team members by genuinely acknowledging their feelings and expressing your understanding and support.

Share your own emotions and experiences: By being open and vulnerable about your own emotions and experiences, you can create a more empathetic environment that encourages others to do the same.

Practice empathetic listening: During conversations, concentrate on understanding the other person's emotions and point of view. Validate their feelings and show genuine concern for their situation.

Cultivate a culture of empathy: Encourage team members to practice empathy and support each other, fostering an atmosphere of understanding and connection.

To sum up, empathy plays a crucial role in effective leadership, allowing us to form deeper connections with others and foster a collaborative and supportive atmosphere. By implementing the strategies and suggestions provided in this chapter, you can strengthen your empathetic leadership skills and build relationships that are more impactful with your team members and colleagues.

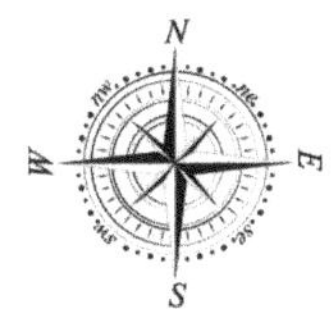

Chapter 4

Building Trust The Foundation of Effective Relationships And World-Changing Leadership

"Honesty is the first chapter in the book of wisdom."
– Buddha

Trust is the foundation of any successful relationship, whether it is personal or professional. In the context of leadership, trust is essential for fostering collaboration, promoting open communication, and driving team performance. Moreover, trust serves as a catalyst for change, empowering leaders and their teams to create lasting, positive impacts on the world. In this chapter, we will explore the importance of trust in transformational leadership, identify strategies for building trust, and offer practical tips for cultivating trust within your team as you work together to shape a better future.

The Role of Trust in World-Changing Leadership

Trust is a vital component of transformational leadership, which aims to inspire and empower others to achieve extraordinary results and make meaningful, lasting change. When trust is established, team members are more likely to share their ideas, take risks, and invest in the collective success of the group. Trust also leads to greater loyalty, commitment, and engagement among team members, which ultimately translates into improved performance and the ability to overcome challenges and create lasting change.

Trust is the driving force behind world-changing leaders, allowing them to inspire others and build resilient, high-performing teams that can tackle complex problems and shape a better future. By cultivating trust, you become a more influential and effective leader, capable of rallying your team around a shared vision and motivating them to pursue ambitious goals.

Strategies for Building Trust and Inspiring Change

Share your vision: Communicate your vision for a better world, detailing how your team's work contributes to that goal. By clearly articulating the impact you seek to make, you inspire your team members to believe in the mission and work toward creating lasting change.

Be transparent and honest: Openly sharing information, being truthful about challenges and opportunities, and admitting when you do not have all the answers are key aspects of building trust. By being transparent and honest, you demonstrate your integrity and create an environment where others feel comfortable doing the same.

Keep your promises: Following through on your commitments is a powerful way to build trust. When you consistently deliver on your promises, you prove your reliability and demonstrate that you can be depended upon.

Show genuine care and concern: Actively demonstrating care and concern for your team members' well-being, both personally and professionally, fosters trust and loyalty. By taking the time to understand their needs, challenges, and aspirations, you show that you value them as individuals, not just as employees.

In conclusion, trust is the cornerstone of world-changing leadership, enabling you to create an environment where your team can thrive and achieve their full potential. By implementing the strategies and tips presented in this chapter, you can strengthen the bonds of trust within your team and drive success in your pursuit of lasting, positive change. Together, you and your team can reshape the world, making it a better place for future generations.

Chapter 5

Fostering Open Communication Encouraging Transparency and Honesty

Introduction

Open communication is essential for effective leadership and living. It is the foundation for creating a transparent, collaborative, and engaged work environment that fosters creativity, innovation, and trust. In this chapter, we will explore the importance of open communication, discuss strategies for fostering transparency and honesty, and offer practical tips for creating a culture of open communication within your team.

The Importance of Open Communication in Leadership

A culture of open communication encourages team members to share their thoughts, ideas, and concerns without fear of retribution or judgment. This exchange of information and ideas allows for better decision-making, problem solving, and innovation. Open communication also contributes to the following benefits:

Improved trust: Open communication builds trust by promoting transparency and honesty. When team members feel safe to share their thoughts and concerns, they are more likely to trust their leader and each other.

Higher engagement: When team members feel heard and valued, they become more engaged in their work and are more likely to contribute their best efforts.

Enhanced collaboration: Open communication fosters a collaborative environment where team members are encouraged to work together, share ideas, and support one another in achieving shared goals.

Strategies for Fostering Open Communication

Model transparency and honesty: As a leader, demonstrate openness by sharing relevant information, being honest about challenges and opportunities, and admitting when you do not have all the answers. This sets the tone for your team and encourages them to be transparent and honest as well.

Actively listen: When team members share their thoughts and ideas, make sure to listen attentively and respond thoughtfully. This demonstrates that you value their input and encourages them to continue sharing.

Encourage feedback: Create opportunities for team members to provide feedback on projects, processes, and leadership. This can be done through regular meetings, anonymous surveys, or one-on-one conversations.

Promote a safe environment: Ensure your team members feel safe to express their thoughts, ideas, and concerns without fear of retribution. Address any issues that arise promptly and fairly to maintain a positive work environment.

Be approachable: Make yourself available for conversations and be open to discussing any concerns or ideas that team members may have. Your approachability and willingness to engage in dialogue will encourage more open communication within your team.

Practical Tips for Creating a Culture of Open Communication

Schedule regular team meetings: Establish a routine for team meetings, where team members can share updates, ask questions, and provide feedback.

Provide multiple channels for communication: Offer various methods for team members to communicate, such as email, instant messaging, and face-to-face conversations.

Recognize and reward openness: Acknowledge and appreciate team members who demonstrate transparency and honesty in their communication. This recognition reinforces the importance of open communication and encourages others to follow suit.

Offer training and development: Provide training and resources on effective communication skills, active listening, and giving and receiving feedback. This empowers team members to communicate more effectively and confidently.

In conclusion, fostering open communication is essential for building trust, promoting collaboration, and driving team performance. By implementing the strategies and tips outlined in this chapter, you can create a culture of transparency and honesty within your team, enabling them to work together more effectively, innovate, and achieve greater success.

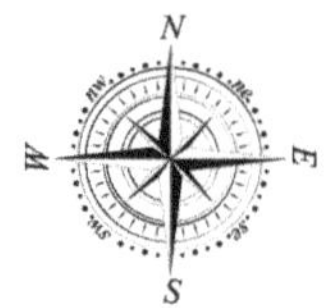

Chapter 6

Leading with Humility Recognizing the Value of Others

Humility is the solid foundation of all virtues.

– Confucius

In this chapter, we will delve into the significance of leading with humility and appreciating the value that others contribute. Successful leadership is not merely about possessing all the answers or asserting authority over others; it is about recognizing the importance of humility, appreciating the strengths of your team members, and understanding that their unique perspectives and contributions can lead to greater success.

A humble leader understands that no one person has all the knowledge or skills needed to solve every problem or seize every opportunity. They recognize that true wisdom comes from acknowledging the expertise and insights of those around them. This humble approach fosters collaboration, drives innovation, and creates an environment where everyone feels valued and empowered to contribute their best work.

When a leader embraces humility, they send a powerful message to their team: "I am here to serve and support you, not merely to command and control." This mindset inspires loyalty, trust, and dedication among team members, as they know their leader genuinely cares about their growth and success.

Here are some essential aspects of leading with humility:

Active Listening: Humble leaders truly listen to their team members, taking the time to understand their thoughts, feelings, and ideas. By doing so, they demonstrate respect and create a safe space for open communication.

Empowering Others: A humble leader encourages team members to take ownership of their work, make decisions, and develop their skills. This trust empowers individuals to grow and achieve their full potential.

Admitting Mistakes: Humble leaders are willing to admit when they are wrong, learn from their mistakes, and seek guidance when needed. This vulnerability fosters an environment where everyone can learn from their missteps and grow together.

Appreciating Diversity: A leader with humility recognizes the value of diverse perspectives and experiences, appreciating the unique qualities each person brings to the team. This appreciation leads to more innovative solutions and a more inclusive work environment.

Giving Credit Where It's due: Humble leaders celebrate the achievements of their team members, recognizing the contributions of each individual. This acknowledgment boosts morale and motivates team members to continue striving for excellence.

In conclusion, leading with humility is a powerful and transformative approach to leadership. By recognizing the value of others, actively listening, empowering team members, admitting mistakes, appreciating diversity, and giving credit where it's due, leaders can create a supportive and thriving environment where everyone can grow and achieve success. Embracing humility as a leader is not a sign of weakness, but rather a demonstration of strength and wisdom, setting the stage for integrity-driven success.

Chapter 7

Demonstrating Respect Honoring the Dignity of Every Individual

We should all consider each other as human beings,
and we should respect each other.

– Malala Yousafzai

The power of respect in leadership is often underestimated, yet it serves as a vital ingredient in building strong relationships, fostering a positive work environment, and achieving organizational goals. Demonstrating respect is not just a moral obligation, but also a key factor in attaining integrity-driven success. In this chapter, we delve into the importance of respecting others and explore the ways leaders can honor the dignity of every individual.

Respect lies at the heart of successful leadership. It is about recognizing the inherent value and worth of each person, irrespective of their role, background, or beliefs. When leaders show respect, they create a foundation of trust, cooperation, and engagement, enabling team members to contribute their best work.

Here are some powerful ways to embody respect as a leader:

Treating Everyone Equally: A respectful leader avoids discrimination or favoritism based on factors such as race, gender, age, or social status. They treat everyone fairly, acknowledging that everyone deserves dignity and respect.

Valuing Opinions and Ideas: Respecting others means appreciating their opinions and ideas, even when they differ from your own. Encourage open communication, actively listen, and provide constructive feedback, fostering an environment where everyone feels heard and valued.

Acknowledging Efforts and Achievements: Respectful leaders recognize the hard work and accomplishments of their team members. They celebrate successes, both big and small, and express gratitude for each person's contributions to the team.

Providing Support and Encouragement: A respectful leader understands the importance of supporting their team members, both personally and professionally. They offer guidance, encouragement, and resources to help individuals overcome challenges and reach their full potential.

Practicing Empathy and Compassion: Respecting others involves understanding their emotions, perspectives, and struggles. By practicing empathy and compassion, leaders can connect with their team members on a deeper level, fostering stronger relationships and a more cohesive team dynamic.

Promoting Inclusivity and Diversity: A respectful leader embraces diversity and actively works to create an inclusive environment where everyone feels welcome and valued. This commitment to inclusivity fosters a sense of belonging and enables team members to bring their unique strengths to the table.

By embracing respect as a foundational principle of leadership, you can create a thriving environment built on trust, collaboration, and mutual respect. Respecting others is essential to achieving integrity-driven success, and it will inspire those around you to strive for greatness, both individually and as a team. Lead with respect, and you will leave an indelible mark on the lives of those you touch.

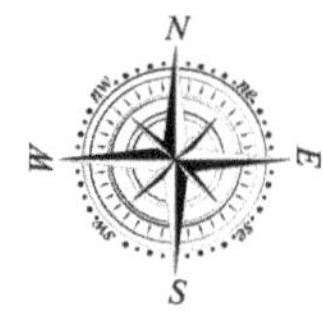

Chapter 8

Practicing Gratitude Appreciating the Contributions of Others

---

"Gratitude makes sense of our past, brings peace for today, and creates a vision for tomorrow."

– Melody Beattie

Gratitude is a powerful force that can transform our lives and the lives of those around us. It enables us to recognize and appreciate the contributions of others, fostering a sense of connection and belonging. When we practice gratitude as leaders, we create an environment where everyone feels valued and respected, which in turn inspires loyalty, trust, and collaboration. In this chapter, we will explore the importance of gratitude, how it contributes to integrity-driven success, and how you can cultivate it in your leadership journey.

A grateful leader sees the world through a lens of appreciation. They recognize that their success is not solely a product of their own efforts, but also the result of the support, hard work, and dedication of others. This recognition allows them to be more open, humble, and receptive to the ideas and input of their team members. Gratitude is a key element of building strong relationships, as it fosters empathy, understanding, and compassion.

Gratitude also serves as a reminder to focus on the positives in our lives. It helps us shift our attention away from our problems and challenges, and instead, concentrate on the countless blessings and opportunities we have. This shift in focus empowers us to face difficulties with greater resilience and to make more thoughtful decisions based on a well-rounded perspective.

To cultivate gratitude in your leadership, consider implementing the following practices:

Keep a gratitude journal: Take a few minutes each day to write down the things you are grateful for, both in your personal life and as a leader. This simple practice can help you stay focused on the positives and reinforce your appreciation for the people and experiences that contribute to your success.

Express appreciation regularly: Make it a point to thank your team members for their hard work, ideas, and dedication. A simple "thank you" can go a long way in making someone feel valued and appreciated. Recognize and celebrate their achievements, both individually and as a team.

Reflect on your blessings: During challenging times, pause and remind yourself of the good things in your life. Acknowledge the support and encouragement you receive from others, and remind yourself of the progress you have made as a leader.

Encourage a culture of gratitude: Foster an environment where team members express gratitude to one another. You can create opportunities for this by initiating team-building activities, holding regular gratitude-sharing sessions, or simply modeling the behavior yourself.

As we conclude this chapter, remember that gratitude is a powerful force that can strengthen your relationships, enhance your leadership, and contribute to your integrity-driven success. By practicing gratitude, you will not only enrich your own life but also inspire those around you to embrace a more positive, collaborative, and fulfilling way of working together.

Chapter 9

Embodying Servant Leadership Putting the Needs of Others First

---

"The ear of the leader must ring with the voices of the people."
– Woodrow Wilson

Servant leadership is a powerful approach to leadership that focuses on the well-being and growth of those being led. It is a philosophy that emphasizes empathy, listening, and empowering others to achieve their full potential. By adopting a servant leadership mindset, you commit to putting the needs of others first and to fostering an environment where everyone thrives. In this chapter, we will delve into the core principles of servant leadership and how embracing this approach can contribute to integrity-driven success.

At the heart of servant leadership is the belief that the most effective leaders prioritize the well-being of their team members. They recognize that their role is not to command or control but to support, mentor, and guide. By genuinely caring for the needs of others, servant leaders inspire loyalty, trust, and collaboration within their teams.

To embody servant leadership, consider incorporating the following principles into your approach:

Active listening: Give your full attention to the thoughts and concerns of your team members. Listen with empathy, and seek to understand their perspectives without judgment. This will not only help you build stronger connections but also enable you to make more informed decisions based on their input.

Empathy: Cultivate the ability to understand and share the feelings of others. When you empathize with your team members, you demonstrate that you value them as individuals and recognize the importance of their experiences.

Empowerment: Encourage your team members to take ownership of their work and to develop their skills and abilities. Provide them with the resources, support, and opportunities they need to grow and succeed in their roles.

Humility: Recognize that you do not have all the answers and that you can learn from your team members. Be open to feedback and willing to admit when you have made a mistake. This humility will foster an environment where everyone feels comfortable sharing his or her ideas and contributing to the team's success.

Commitment to the growth of others: Invest in the personal and professional development of your team members. Offer mentorship, training, and other growth opportunities that will help them excel in their roles and achieve their long-term goals.

By embracing servant leadership, you demonstrate a commitment to the well-being and success of your team members. This approach not only aligns with the principles of integrity-driven success but also fosters a positive, supportive work environment where everyone can thrive. As you continue your journey as a leader, remember that the greatest impact you can make is by putting the needs of others first and empowering them to reach their full potential.

Chapter 10

Pursuing Lifelong Learning Continuously Seeking Knowledge and Growth

Lifelong learning is the continuous pursuit of knowledge and personal growth, which is essential for maintaining a competitive edge in today's rapidly evolving world. By committing to lifelong learning, you demonstrate that you value self-improvement, adaptability, and innovation, all of which contribute to integrity-driven success. In this chapter, we will explore the benefits of lifelong learning and discuss strategies for cultivating a growth mindset and a love for continuous learning.

Embracing lifelong learning brings numerous benefits, including:

Enhanced adaptability: As the world around us changes at an unprecedented pace, the ability to adapt and learn new skills is critical. Lifelong learners are better equipped to navigate the challenges that arise and seize new opportunities.

Increased self-confidence: Continuously acquiring new knowledge and skills boosts your self-confidence, empowering you to take on challenges and pursue your goals with conviction.

Improved decision-making: The more you learn, the better equipped you are to make informed decisions. Lifelong learners are better able to assess situations, gather information, and analyze the consequences of their choices.

Greater innovation: Lifelong learning fosters creativity and innovation, as it enables you to approach problems with fresh perspectives and generate new ideas.

Personal fulfillment: The process of learning and growing is intrinsically rewarding and can bring a deep sense of satisfaction and purpose to your life.

To cultivate a lifelong learning mindset, consider adopting the following strategies:

Set clear goals: Identify specific areas in which you want to develop your knowledge and skills. Establish clear, attainable goals and commit to making steady progress toward them.

Embrace curiosity: Cultivate a sense of curiosity and wonder about the world around you. Seek out new experiences, ask questions, and explore new ideas to fuel your desire to learn.

Surround yourself with like-minded individuals: Build relationships with people who share your passion for learning and personal growth. These connections can provide inspiration, support, and valuable insights as you pursue your learning journey.

Leverage diverse learning resources: Take advantage of the wealth of learning opportunities available, from books and podcasts to online courses and workshops. Diversify your learning resources to gain a well-rounded understanding of your chosen subject matter.

Reflect on your progress: Regularly assess your progress and reflect on your learning experiences. Identify areas in which you can improve and celebrate your achievements.

By committing to lifelong learning, you invest in your personal growth and demonstrate your dedication to integrity-driven success. As a leader, you also set a powerful example for your team members, inspiring them to pursue their own learning journeys and fostering a culture of continuous improvement.

Chapter 11

Encouraging Innovation Inspiring Creativity and Ingenuity

"What is now proved was once only imagined."
–William Blake

Innovation is the lifeblood of progress and success, both in business and in personal development. As a leader who values integrity-driven success, fostering an environment that encourages creativity and ingenuity is essential. In this chapter, we will discuss the importance of innovation and explore strategies for inspiring and nurturing it within your team or organization.

The benefits of encouraging innovation include:

Increased competitiveness: In a constantly evolving world, organizations that prioritize innovation are better equipped to adapt, grow, and maintain a competitive advantage.

Enhanced problem solving: Creativity and ingenuity are essential for tackling complex challenges and finding innovative solutions. By fostering an innovative mindset, you enable your team to approach problems from new perspectives and generate breakthrough ideas.

Greater employee engagement: When employees feel empowered to think creatively and contribute their ideas, they are more likely to be engaged and invested in their work, which leads to increased productivity and job satisfaction.

Stronger collaboration: Innovative environments often encourage collaboration and open communication, which can result in better teamwork and more effective problem-solving.

To inspire and cultivate innovation, consider the following strategies:

Embrace a growth mindset: Encourage a growth mindset in yourself and your team members by celebrating effort, learning from setbacks, and embracing challenges as opportunities for growth.

Foster a culture of psychological safety: Create an environment where employees feel safe to express their ideas and take risks without fear of judgment or retribution. Encourage open communication and provide constructive feedback.

Encourage curiosity and experimentation: Emphasize the importance of curiosity and exploration in the pursuit of innovation. Provide opportunities for team members to experiment with new ideas and approaches.

Recognize and reward innovation: Acknowledge and celebrate the creative contributions of your team members. By recognizing and rewarding innovation, you reinforce its value and motivate others to think creatively.

Provide resources and support: Ensure your team has access to the necessary resources, tools, and support to explore new ideas and bring them to fruition.

As a leader committed to integrity-driven success, encouraging innovation is not only vital for your organization's growth but also for the personal growth of your team members. By fostering an environment that values creativity and ingenuity, you empower your team to reach new heights and make a lasting impact.

Chapter 12

Setting Clear Expectations Providing Direction and Focus

Efforts and courage are not enough without purpose and direction.

– John F. Kennedy

Welcome to Chapter 12 of our journey towards becoming exceptional leaders. Today, we will be discussing one of the most crucial aspects of leadership - setting clear expectations. As leaders, it is our responsibility to provide direction and focus to our teams, guiding them towards a shared vision and common goal. By setting clear expectations, we can ensure that our team members understand their roles and responsibilities, know what is expected of them, and have a clear roadmap to success.

The Importance of Setting Clear Expectations

Setting clear expectations is essential for effective leadership, as it lays the foundation for a high-performing team. When expectations are unclear or undefined, team members may lack direction, motivation, and a sense of purpose, leading to confusion, disengagement, and ultimately, poor performance. On the other hand, when expectations are clearly communicated and understood, team members are more likely to be engaged, motivated, and aligned with the overall goals of the organization.

Strategies for Setting Clear Expectations

Define goals and objectives: Begin by defining clear, specific, and measurable goals and objectives that align with the overall mission and vision of the organization. Break these goals down into manageable, actionable steps, and clearly communicate them to your team members.

Establish roles and responsibilities: Clearly define the roles and responsibilities of each team member, ensuring that everyone understands their individual contributions and how they fit into the larger picture. This will help to eliminate confusion and duplication of effort, and allow team members to focus on their specific areas of expertise.

Communicate regularly: Regular communication is key to setting and maintaining clear expectations. Schedule regular check-ins and team meetings to ensure that everyone is on the same page, and provide timely feedback and guidance to help team members stay on track.

Lead by example: As a leader, it is important to model the behavior and attitude that you expect from your team members. By leading by example, you can inspire your team to perform at their best and set the tone for a culture of excellence.

Actionable Tips for Setting Clear Expectations

Be consistent: Consistency is essential for setting clear expectations. Ensure that your actions and communications are aligned with the expectations you have set, and hold yourself and others accountable for meeting these expectations.

Provide feedback: Regularly provide feedback and recognition to your team members, highlighting areas of success and opportunities for improvement. This will help to keep everyone on track and motivated to achieve his or her goals.

Adjust as needed: Finally, remember that setting clear expectations is an ongoing process. Be open to feedback and adjust your approach as needed to ensure that everyone is aligned with the overall goals of the organization.

Setting clear expectations is a critical aspect of effective integrity-driven leadership, providing direction, focus, and motivation to your team members. By following the strategies and tips outlined in this chapter, you can ensure that your team is aligned with the overall mission and vision of the organization, and poised for success. Keep in mind that setting clear expectations is an ongoing process that requires consistent effort and attention, but with dedication and perseverance, you can lead your team towards greatness.

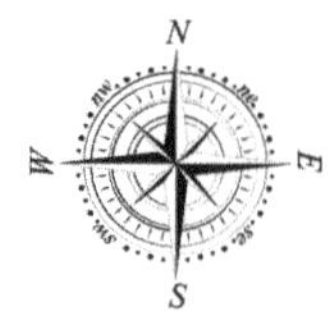

Chapter 13

Creating a Shared Vision: Aligning Team Efforts towards a Common Goal

Welcome to Chapter 13 of "The Moral Compass: 48 Principles for Achieving Integrity-Driven Success." In this chapter, we will explore the importance of creating a shared vision and aligning team efforts towards a common goal. A shared vision is a powerful tool that can transform a group of individuals into a highly effective team, capable of achieving incredible results.

Throughout history, we have seen the power of a shared vision in action. Just think of the Wright Brothers, who had a vision of powered flight and worked tirelessly to make it a reality. On the other hand, consider Martin Luther King Jr., whose dream of a world free from discrimination and inequality inspired millions of people to take action towards achieving that vision.

A shared vision provides a clear direction and purpose for a team, aligning their efforts towards a common goal. It creates a sense of unity, fosters collaboration and creativity, and motivates team members to work together towards a shared purpose.

Here are some strategies for creating a shared vision and aligning team efforts towards a common goal:

Define a clear purpose: A shared vision starts with a clear and compelling purpose. Define a purpose that resonates with your team members and inspires them to work towards a common goal.

Communicate the vision: Communicate the vision in a clear and concise way, making sure everyone understands the purpose, goals, and expectations. This helps to create a sense of shared understanding and ownership of the vision.

Create a plan: Develop a plan that outlines the steps needed to achieve the shared vision. Involve team members in the planning process, ensuring everyone is committed to the vision and has a clear understanding of their role in achieving it.

Build a culture of trust: A shared vision requires trust and collaboration. Build a culture of trust within your team by creating a safe and supportive environment where team members feel valued and respected.

Celebrate progress: Celebrate progress towards the shared vision, no matter how small. This helps to create a sense of momentum and reinforces the team's commitment to the vision.

By creating a shared vision and aligning team efforts towards a common goal, you can transform your team into a highly effective and motivated group of individuals. Just like the Wright Brothers and Martin Luther King Jr., you can inspire your team to achieve incredible results by sharing a clear and compelling vision.

So, start by defining a clear purpose, communicating the vision, and building a culture of trust. Then, develop a plan and celebrate progress along the way. By following these strategies, you can lead your team towards a shared vision and achieve remarkable success.

Chapter 14

Ignite the Fire Within Unleashing Your Team's Limitless Potential

"Continuous effort, not strength or intelligence is the key to unlocking our potential."

– Winston Churchill

I magine a world where each individual on your team feels energized, motivated, and inspired to bring their best selves to work every single day. As a leader, you have the power to make this dream a reality by empowering your team members to discover their unique talents, take ownership of their work, and ultimately, contribute to your organization's unstoppable success. In this electrifying chapter, we will dive deep into the essence of empowering leadership, uncover the strategies to create a thriving environment, and provide you with actionable tips to ignite the fire within your team.

The Power of Empowering Leadership

By embracing the role of an empowering leader, you unlock the incredible potential that lies within each member of your team. When you empower others, you:

Fuel motivation and engagement: Empowerment ignites a burning desire for success, fostering a sense of ownership and pride in one's work, leading to sky-high levels of motivation and engagement.

Spark innovation and creativity: When team members feel empowered, they dare to take risks, think outside the box, and unleash their creative genius, driving your organization to the forefront of success.

Amplify team performance: Empowered teams outshine the rest, as individuals take responsibility for their work and collaborate effectively, achieving extraordinary results.

Cultivate future leaders: Empowering others is the catalyst for identifying and nurturing the next generation of trailblazing leaders, ensuring your organization's continued growth and success.

Strategies to Ignite an Empowering Environment

Build a rock-solid foundation of trust: Trust is the cornerstone of empowerment. Show your unwavering belief in your team's abilities by granting them autonomy and responsibility. Foster open communication and transparency to fortify trust among team members.

Equip your team for success: Provide your team with the essential tools, resources, and support they need to excel. Offer transformative training, coaching, and mentorship to guide them in conquering challenges and honing their skills.

Illuminate clear expectations and goals: Communicate your expectations with crystal-clear clarity and set awe-inspiring goals for your team. Establish a shared vision and ensure that members grasp their individual responsibilities in bringing that vision to life.

Champion collaboration and teamwork: Cultivate an environment where collaboration thrives, and team members feel comfortable sharing ideas, seeking assistance, and joining forces to tackle problems.

Actionable Tips to Ignite the Fire within Your Team

Delegate with purpose and precision: Delegate tasks and responsibilities to your team members based on their unique strengths, passions, and development goals. Offer guidance and support while also granting them the autonomy to make decisions and take charge of their work.

Celebrate triumphs and victories: Applaud and honor the achievements of your team members, both individually and collectively. This recognition fuels morale, reinforces positive behavior, and propels your team to even greater heights.

Deliver transformative feedback and coaching: Offer life-changing feedback and coaching to help your team members evolve and excel in their roles. Create a feedback-rich environment where everyone learns and grows from both their successes and failures.

Adapt your leadership style like a chameleon: Recognize that each team member may require a unique leadership approach to feel empowered. Tailor your style based on individual needs and preferences to ensure you effectively support and motivate each team member.

In conclusion, empowering others is a vital aspect of extraordinary leadership, as it enables your team to reach its full potential and make a monumental impact on your organization's success. By implementing the strategies and tips outlined in this thrilling chapter, you can create an empowering environment that fuels motivation, innovation, and growth. Get ready to ignite the fire within your team and watch them soar to unprecedented heights, achieving remarkable performance and redefining the limits of what is possible.

Remember, the journey of empowering leadership is a thrilling adventure, not a one-time event. Keep the flame alive by continuously nurturing trust, providing support, and recognizing the hard work and dedication of your team members. Stay committed to fostering a culture that encourages collaboration, creativity, and growth. In addition, most importantly, believe in your team and in their limitless potential to create lasting, meaningful change.

Together, you and your team can conquer the world, break through barriers, and reach the pinnacle of success. Embrace your role as an empowering leader and unleash the extraordinary power that lies within each member of your team. Let the fire burn brightly, and watch as your organization achieves unparalleled success and leaves a lasting legacy for generations to come.

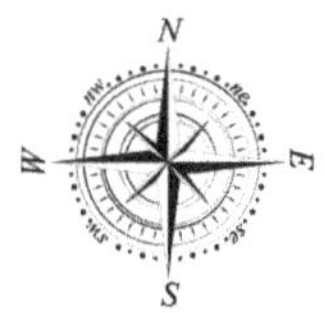

Chapter 15

Nurturing Collaboration Fostering a Culture of Teamwork

In today's dynamic and interconnected world, collaboration is the lifeblood of success. It is the magical ingredient that transforms a group of individuals into a high-performing, unstoppable team. In this inspiring chapter, we will explore the importance of nurturing collaboration, unveil strategies for fostering a culture of teamwork, and provide you with actionable tips to help you create an environment where collaboration thrives.

The Power of Collaboration

When people come together, share ideas, and work towards a common goal, they can achieve far more than they could individually. The benefits of collaboration are manifold:

Enhanced problem solving: A diverse team brings together a wealth of unique perspectives, experiences, and skills, making it easier to tackle complex challenges and find innovative solutions.

Increased creativity: Collaboration encourages the free flow of ideas, sparking creativity and driving innovation.

Greater efficiency: Collaborative teams can accomplish tasks more quickly and effectively, leveraging the strengths of each member and overcoming obstacles with ease.

Stronger relationships: When people work together, they build trust, develop a deeper understanding of one another, and forge lasting connections.

Strategies for Fostering a Culture of Teamwork

Communicate a clear vision: Share your team's purpose and objectives, ensuring that everyone understands the common goal and how their individual contributions fit into the bigger picture.

Establish psychological safety: Create an environment where team members feel comfortable voicing their opinions, asking questions, and taking risks without fear of judgment or retribution.

Encourage diverse perspectives: Embrace and celebrate the unique backgrounds, experiences, and viewpoints of your team members. Encourage open and respectful discussions, and leverage these diverse perspectives to drive innovation and growth.

Develop team-building activities: Plan regular team-building activities, both in and outside the workplace, to strengthen relationships, enhance communication, and promote a sense of camaraderie.

Actionable Tips for Nurturing Collaboration

Model collaborative behavior: As a leader, set the tone for collaboration by actively seeking input from your team, listening attentively, and encouraging open communication.

Foster cross-functional collaboration: Encourage collaboration between different departments or functional areas within your organization. This cross-pollination of ideas can lead to innovative solutions and increased efficiency.

Recognize and reward teamwork: Celebrate collaborative achievements, both big and small. Recognize and reward those who contribute to the team's success, reinforcing the value of collaboration and teamwork.

Provide tools and resources: Equip your team with the tools and resources they need to collaborate effectively, such as digital platforms for communication and project management, as well as physical spaces designed to facilitate teamwork.

In conclusion, nurturing collaboration is a vital aspect of effective leadership, as it unlocks the full potential of your team and paves the way for success. By implementing the strategies and tips outlined in this chapter, you can foster a culture of teamwork that fuels creativity, enhances problem-solving, and propels your organization towards its goals. Remember, collaboration is not just a skill to be developed; it is a mindset to be embraced and celebrated. Together, you and your team can achieve greatness and leave an indelible mark on the world.

Chapter 16

Celebrating Diversity Embracing Different Perspectives and Experiences

The richness of human experience is a treasure trove that can ignite the flames of innovation and propel us toward new heights of achievement. Embrace the beauty of diversity and unlock the boundless potential of your team. In this inspiring chapter, we will delve into the power of diversity, share stories of organizations that have harnessed its potential, and provide you with actionable tips to create an environment where everyone's unique strengths are valued and nurtured.

The Transformative Power of Diversity

Diversity is a remarkable force that can unleash creativity, strengthen problem solving, and enhance adaptability. When we come together as a tapestry of different backgrounds, experiences, and perspectives, we create a dynamic synergy that drives innovation and growth. To illustrate the power of diversity, let's explore the story of NASA's "Hidden Figures."

In the early days of the US space program, NASA faced enormous challenges in their quest to land a man on the moon. It was the diverse talents and perspectives of the team of African American female mathematicians - Katherine

Johnson, Dorothy Vaughan, and Mary Jackson - that helped NASA overcome these challenges and make history. These trailblazing women defied the societal norms of their time and proved that when we embrace diversity, we can achieve the seemingly impossible (Shetterly, 2016).

Strategies for Promoting Inclusivity and Harnessing the Power of Diversity

Share inspiring stories: Regularly share stories of individuals and organizations that have harnessed the power of diversity to achieve remarkable success. These stories can serve as a powerful reminder of the potential that lies within our differences.

Encourage mentoring and reverse mentoring: Pair team members from different backgrounds, generations, or areas of expertise to facilitate learning, understanding, and appreciation for each other's unique perspectives and experiences.

Provide opportunities for diverse teams to tackle high-impact projects: Empower teams with diverse members to take on challenging projects and initiatives, demonstrating the value and strength that diversity brings to problem solving and innovation.

In conclusion, celebrating diversity is a vital principle for integrity-driven success, as it enables your team to unleash its full potential and make a meaningful impact on the world. As we embrace the beauty of our differences and harness the power of diversity, we embark on an extraordinary journey towards greatness. Remember, when we unite our unique strengths, experiences, and perspectives, we create an unstoppable force that can conquer challenges, drive innovation, and leave a lasting legacy of success.

Source:

Shetterly, M. L. (2016). Hidden Figures: The American Dream and the Untold Story of the Black Women Mathematicians Who Helped Win the Space Race. William Morrow & Company.

Chapter 17

Developing Resilience Overcoming Challenges and Adversity

"Enthusiasm is common. Endurance is rare."

– Angela Duckworth

In the face of life's inevitable storms, resilience is the beacon that guides us through the darkness, illuminating our path to personal growth and triumph. Resilience empowers us to embrace adversity, learn from our experiences, and emerge stronger and wiser. In this life-changing chapter, we will delve into the transformative power of resilience, and equip you with practical strategies to help you cultivate unshakable resilience for a fulfilling, integrity-driven life.

The Transformative Power of Resilience

Resilience is a remarkable force that allows us to persevere in the face of setbacks, persistently pursuing our goals and dreams. This quality can be honed, strengthened, and nurtured, shaping our response to adversity and fostering personal growth.

When we cultivate resilience, we:

Embrace change and uncertainty: Resilient individuals are better equipped to navigate life's uncertainties, adapting to new circumstances, and finding creative solutions to problems.

Foster personal growth: Facing adversity with resilience allows us to learn valuable lessons, refine our skills, and strengthen our character.

Cultivate a sense of purpose: Resilience enables us to remain focused on our core values and beliefs, even when confronted with seemingly insurmountable obstacles.

The Inspiring Story of J.K. Rowling

J.K. Rowling's journey to becoming one of the most successful authors of all time is a testament to the power of resilience. Before she penned the beloved Harry Potter series, Rowling faced a series of setbacks, including the loss of her mother, the end of her marriage, and living in poverty as a single mother.

Despite her struggles, Rowling never lost sight of her passion for writing. She persevered, working on the manuscript for the first Harry Potter book in cafes while her baby daughter slept beside her. Her resilience and determination ultimately paid off when "Harry Potter and the Philosopher's Stone" was published, catapulting Rowling to worldwide fame and success.

Practical Strategies for Cultivating Resilience

Embrace a growth mindset: Adopt a mindset that views challenges as opportunities for growth and learning, rather than insurmountable obstacles. Recognize that setbacks can be valuable teachers that help us refine our skills and expand our understanding.

Develop strong support networks: Surround yourself with people who believe in you, encourage you, and help you navigate life's challenges with resilience and grace. Seek out mentors, friends, and loved ones who uplift you and support your growth.

Practice self-compassion: Be kind to yourself when you face setbacks, acknowledging your feelings and recognizing that failure is a natural part of the human experience. Treat yourself with the same care and understanding that you would offer to a friend in a similar situation.

Set realistic goals and celebrate progress: Break down your long-term goals into smaller, achievable milestones, and celebrate your progress along the way. Recognizing and celebrating your accomplishments can bolster your confidence and reinforce your resilience.

Cultivate mindfulness and gratitude: Engage in mindfulness practices, such as meditation and deep breathing, to develop self-awareness and manage stress more effectively. Additionally, focus on the positives in your life and express gratitude for them, even in the face of adversity. This practice can help you maintain perspective and foster resilience.

In conclusion, developing resilience is a vital principle for integrity-driven success, as it enables us to overcome challenges, learn from our experiences, and persistently pursue our goals and dreams. By applying the strategies and insights shared in this chapter, you will be well on your way to cultivating unshakable resilience, empowering you to navigate life's uncertainties

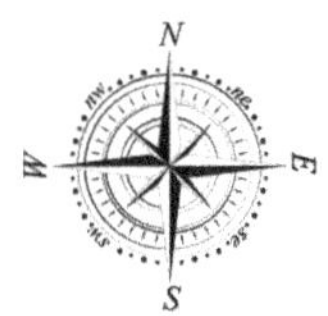

Chapter 18

Practicing Adaptability

Embracing Change and Uncertainty

"The wise adapt themselves to circumstances, as water molds itself to the pitcher."

– Chinese Proverb

As the world continues to evolve at an ever-accelerating pace, adaptability has become a critical skill for thriving in the face of change and uncertainty. To achieve lasting success and personal growth, we must learn to be flexible, open-minded, and receptive to new ideas and perspectives. In this empowering chapter, we will explore the importance of adaptability in our lives, and offer practical strategies to help you cultivate this essential quality for integrity-driven success.

The Importance of Adaptability

Adaptability is the ability to adjust to new situations, learn from experience, and embrace change with an open mind.

By cultivating adaptability, we can:

Navigate the complexities of modern life: In today's fast-paced, ever-changing world, adaptability equips us to deal with the unexpected and find creative solutions to problems.

Foster personal growth: Adaptability enables us to learn from our experiences, expand our skillset, and develop a deeper understanding of ourselves and the world around us.

Enhance our relationships: By being adaptable, we can better understand and accommodate the needs of others, fostering stronger connections and collaborations.

The Inspiring Story of Charles Darwin

Charles Darwin's groundbreaking work in the field of evolutionary biology is a shining example of adaptability in action. Darwin's theory of natural selection, which he developed after years of observation and research, revolutionized the way we understand the natural world and our place within it.

Darwin's adaptability allowed him to challenge prevailing scientific beliefs and embrace new ideas, ultimately leading to the development of his seminal work, "On the Origin of Species." His willingness to revise his thinking and adjust to new information laid the groundwork for modern evolutionary theory and changed the course of scientific history.

Practical Strategies for Cultivating Adaptability

Adopt a growth mindset: Embrace the idea that your abilities and intelligence can be developed through effort, learning, and persistence. A growth mindset will help you remain open to new ideas, experiences, and perspectives.

Foster curiosity and continuous learning: Cultivate a genuine interest in the world around you, seeking out new experiences and opportunities for growth. Stay informed about current events, trends, and advances in your field to remain adaptable and responsive to change.

Practice active listening: Make a conscious effort to listen attentively and openly to the ideas and perspectives of others. Active listening allows us to gain new insights, challenge our assumptions, and adapt our thinking when necessary.

Embrace change and uncertainty: Recognize that change is a natural part of life and that uncertainty can offer valuable opportunities for growth and learning. Instead of resisting change, approach it with an open mind and a willingness to adapt.

Develop problem-solving skills: Strengthen your ability to analyze situations, identify potential solutions, and evaluate the best course of action. Effective problem-solving skills will enable you to adapt to new challenges and navigate the complexities of modern life.

In conclusion, practicing adaptability is a vital principle for integrity-driven success, allowing us to embrace change, learn from our experiences, and thrive in an ever-evolving world. By applying the strategies and insights shared in this chapter, you will be well on your way to cultivating the adaptability necessary for personal growth, meaningful relationships, and lasting success.

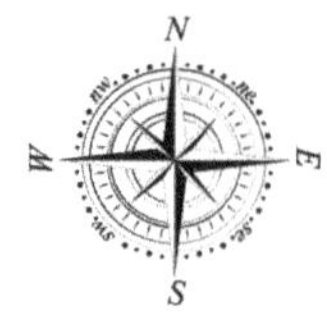

Chapter 19

Cultivating Emotional Intelligence Managing Emotions

In a world where emotional intelligence is increasingly recognized as a powerful asset, cultivating this skill is essential for integrity-driven success. Emotional intelligence, or EQ, is the ability to recognize, understand, and manage our emotions and the emotions of others. In this enlightening chapter, we will explore the importance of emotional intelligence in our lives, and provide practical strategies to help you develop and refine your emotional intelligence for a more fulfilling, emotionally balanced life.

The Importance of Emotional Intelligence

Emotional intelligence is a crucial skill that contributes to our personal and professional success in a variety of ways:

Enhance self-awareness: By developing emotional intelligence, we can better understand our emotions, motivations, and reactions, leading to increased self-awareness and personal growth.

Foster healthy relationships: Emotional intelligence allows us to empathize with others, communicate effectively, and resolve conflicts, resulting in stronger, more satisfying relationships.

Improve decision-making: A heightened EQ enables us to make informed decisions, taking into account both logical and emotional considerations.

Boost performance and productivity: Emotional intelligence equips us with the tools to manage stress, maintain focus, and motivate ourselves and others, leading to enhanced performance and productivity.

The Inspiring Story of Oprah Winfrey

Oprah Winfrey, the world-renowned media mogul and philanthropist, exemplifies emotional intelligence in both her personal and professional life. As a talk show host, Oprah used her exceptional EQ to connect with guests and audiences on a deeply emotional level, creating a space for open, honest, and transformative conversations.

Oprah's ability to empathize with others, communicate effectively, and manage her emotions has been a significant factor in her extraordinary success. Her emotional intelligence has allowed her to inspire millions of people worldwide and make a meaningful impact through her various philanthropic endeavors.

Practical Strategies for Cultivating Emotional Intelligence

Practice self-reflection: Regularly assess your thoughts, feelings, and behaviors to gain a deeper understanding of your emotions and reactions. Journaling, meditation, and mindfulness practices can be helpful tools for self-reflection.

Develop empathy: Cultivate the ability to put yourself in someone else's shoes and understand their feelings and perspectives. Actively listen to others, ask open-ended questions, and validate their emotions to enhance your empathy skills.

Learn to manage stress: Develop healthy coping mechanisms for managing stress and anxiety, such as deep breathing, exercise, or engaging in creative activities. By effectively managing stress, you can maintain emotional balance and make better decisions.

Practice assertive communication: Express your thoughts, feelings, and needs openly and respectfully, while also being receptive to the perspectives of others. Assertive communication fosters mutual understanding and reduces the likelihood of emotional conflicts.

Seek feedback: Regularly solicit feedback from trusted friends, family members, or colleagues to gain insights into your emotional intelligence and identify areas for improvement.

In conclusion, cultivating emotional intelligence is a powerful guiding principle for integrity-driven success, enabling us to navigate our emotions, connect with others, and lead more fulfilling lives. By applying the strategies and insights shared in this chapter, you will be well on your way to developing the emotional intelligence necessary for personal growth, meaningful relationships, and lasting success.

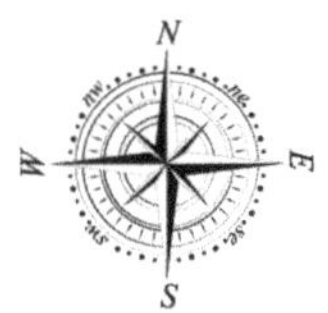

Chapter 20

Leading by Example Modeling the Behavior You Expect from Others

"What you are speaks so loudly, I can't hear what you are saying."

– Ralph Waldo Emerson

One of the most profound ways to inspire and motivate others is by leading through example. As a leader, your actions and behaviors speak volumes, setting the tone for your team and shaping the organizational culture. This chapter delves into the significance of embodying the behaviors you expect from others, sharing captivating examples of influential figures who have done so, and offering valuable guidance to help you become the living embodiment of your values and expectations.

The Power of Leading by Example

When you lead by example, you demonstrate your commitment to the values and principles you champion. This commitment resonates with others, fostering a sense of trust, respect, and admiration. By modeling the behavior you expect, you create an environment where your team members are more likely to follow suit, ultimately contributing to a positive and productive atmosphere.

A Compelling Story of Rosa Parks

Rosa Parks, a courageous civil rights activist, exemplified the power of leading by example. Through her simple but defiant act of refusing to give up her seat on a segregated bus in Montgomery, Alabama, she sparked the Montgomery Bus Boycott and became an inspiration for the Civil Rights Movement. Parks' brave act demonstrated the importance of standing up for what is right, even in the face of adversity, and inspired countless others to join the fight for racial equality.

Guidelines for Embodying the Behaviors You Expect from Others

Clarify your values: Identify the core values and principles that guide your life and leadership, and commit to living in alignment with them. This clarity serves as a foundation for leading by example.

Be consistent: Strive for consistency in your actions and behaviors, ensuring that they align with your values and expectations. Consistency builds trust and credibility, making it more likely that others will follow your lead.

Hold yourself accountable: Take responsibility for your actions and decisions, acknowledging mistakes and learning from them. By holding yourself accountable, you demonstrate the importance of taking ownership and learning from setbacks.

Be transparent: Share your thought processes, challenges, and successes with your team, creating an environment of openness and trust. Transparency enables your team members to better understand your values and expectations and encourages them to follow suit.

Inspire and motivate: Encourage your team members by acknowledging their efforts, celebrating their successes, and providing constructive feedback. By fostering a positive and supportive atmosphere, you inspire others to embody the behaviors you expect.

As you embark on the journey of leading by example, remember that your actions have the power to inspire, motivate, and shape the behaviors of those around you. By consciously embodying the values and expectations, you hold dear, you will not only cultivate a thriving team but also leave a lasting impact on the lives of the people you touch. Embrace the responsibility and the opportunity that comes with leading by example, and watch as your influence transforms your team and the world around you.

Chapter 21

Establishing Accountability Holding Yourself and Others Responsible

---

*"If you're going to be a leader, you're not going to please everybody.
You have to hold people accountable, even if you have that moment
of being uncomfortable."*

– Kobe Bryant

Accountability is a critical aspect of effective leadership and team performance. By holding ourselves and others accountable for our actions and decisions, we create an environment of trust, responsibility, and continuous improvement. In this transformative chapter, we will examine the importance of accountability, share compelling examples of leaders who have embraced this principle, and offer valuable tips to help you establish a culture of accountability within your team.

The Importance of Accountability

Accountability is the willingness to accept responsibility for our actions and their consequences.

Embracing accountability has a powerful impact on our personal and professional lives:

Builds trust: When we hold ourselves and others accountable, we create an atmosphere of trust and reliability, fostering strong relationships with our team members and stakeholders.

Encourages personal growth: Accountability pushes us to learn from our mistakes, reflect on our actions, and grow both personally and professionally.

Enhances team performance: A culture of accountability drives team members to take ownership of their responsibilities and strive for excellence, leading to increased productivity and performance.

Promotes ethical behavior: When accountability is a priority, individuals are more likely to act with integrity, upholding the values and principles that guide their actions.

The Inspiring Story of Malala Yousafzai

Malala Yousafzai, the youngest Nobel Peace Prize laureate, is a shining example of personal accountability. Despite being targeted by the Taliban for advocating for girls' education, Malala refused to be silenced. Instead, she held herself accountable for her beliefs and used her experience to raise awareness about the importance of education for girls worldwide. Malala's dedication to her cause and her willingness to take responsibility for her actions have inspired millions and demonstrated the power of accountability.

Tips for Establishing Accountability within Your Team

Set clear expectations: Clearly communicate your expectations and goals to your team, ensuring that everyone understands their roles and responsibilities.

Provide the necessary resources: Equip your team with the tools, information, and support they need to meet their responsibilities and achieve their goals.

Create a feedback loop: Establish regular check-ins and performance reviews to monitor progress, provide constructive feedback, and address any obstacles or challenges.

Foster open communication: Encourage honest and transparent communication within your team, creating a safe space for individuals to discuss their concerns, ask questions, and share their ideas.

Hold yourself accountable: As a leader, model the behavior you expect from others by holding yourself accountable for your actions, decisions, and performance. This sets a powerful example for your team and demonstrates your commitment to accountability.

In conclusion, establishing accountability is a vital guiding principle for integrity-driven success. By holding ourselves and others responsible for our actions and their consequences, we can create an environment of trust, responsibility, and continuous improvement. Embrace the power of accountability in your leadership journey, and watch as your team thrives and achieves new heights of success.

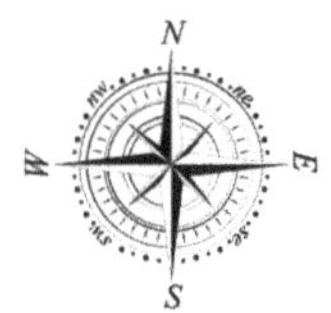

Chapter 22

Mastering the Art of Decision-Making Unleashing the Power of Logic and Intuition

*"Nothing is more difficult, and therefore more precious,
than to be able to decide."*

– Napoleon Bonaparte

The ability to make wise decisions is a hallmark of exceptional leaders. In this ever-changing world, the stakes are high, and the consequences of our choices can be far-reaching. Brian Tracy, a renowned author and motivational speaker, once said, "Decisiveness is a characteristic of high-performing men and women. Almost any decision is better than no decision at all." So, how can we develop this essential leadership skill? By striking the perfect balance between logic and intuition.

Embrace the Science of Logic

Logical thinking is the foundation of effective decision-making. It enables us to analyze information, evaluate alternatives, and predict potential outcomes.

To harness the power of logic, consider these three key strategies:

Gather relevant information: Arm yourself with the necessary data and insights to make informed decisions. Seek out diverse sources to ensure a comprehensive understanding of the situation.

Evaluate alternatives: Weigh the pros and cons of each option, considering the potential consequences and the alignment with your values and goals.

Develop a systematic approach: Utilize decision-making models and tools, such as decision trees or cost-benefit analysis, to bring structure and objectivity to your decision-making process.

Unlock the Wisdom of Intuition: Intuition is the secret ingredient that adds depth and nuance to our decision-making abilities. It is the whisper of our subconscious, guiding us through our accumulated experiences, instincts, and emotions. To unleash the power of intuition, follow these three steps:

Develop self-awareness: Cultivate a deeper understanding of your values, beliefs, and emotions to enhance your intuitive abilities.

Trust your gut feelings: Learn to recognize and trust the signals your intuition sends, even when they seem to defy logic.

Reflect on past experiences: Use the lessons from previous successes and failures to inform your intuitive decision-making.

Finding the Perfect Balance

To master the art of decision-making, you must learn to seamlessly blend logic and intuition.

Here are three techniques to help you achieve this balance:

Pause and reflect: Before making a decision, take a moment to quiet your mind, allowing your logical and intuitive insights to come together.

Seek diverse perspectives: Consult with trusted colleagues or mentors who bring different viewpoints, experiences, and decision-making styles to the table.

Continuously learn and grow: Embrace a growth mindset by actively seeking new experiences, knowledge, and feedback to refine your decision-making abilities.

As you embark on your journey to becoming a decisive leader, remember that the perfect balance between logic and intuition is within your reach. By combining these two powerful forces, you will unlock the full potential of your decision-making abilities, empowering you to lead with confidence, wisdom, and clarity. So, take a deep breath, trust yourself, and seize the power to make extraordinary decisions that will shape your destiny.

Chapter 23

Conquering Time Unleashing the Power of Prioritization and Focus

As you journey through the world of leadership, one valuable resource stands above the rest – time. It is a limited commodity, and how we use it profoundly impacts our success, both personally and professionally. Time management is the art of prioritizing tasks and allocating our precious moments effectively. When we master this skill, we unlock the door to unparalleled productivity, efficiency, and achievement.

Time is the great equalizer, and every person on this planet shares the same 24 hours each day. The question is, how can we make the most of it? In this chapter, we will explore the secrets to time management success and provide you with the strategies and tools you need to maximize your potential.

The Power of Prioritization

The essence of time management lies in our ability to prioritize tasks, focusing our energy on what truly matters. By distinguishing between the important and the urgent, the essential and the trivial, we can carve out the path to success.

Here are four strategies to master the art of prioritization:

Identify your goals: To prioritize effectively, you must first establish your short-term and long-term goals. Determine what you want to accomplish, and let these objectives guide your decision-making.

Embrace the Pareto Principle: Also known as the 80/20 rule, the Pareto Principle suggests that 80% of our results come from 20% of our efforts. Identify the high-impact tasks that will yield the greatest results and prioritize them accordingly.

Create a daily to-do list: Each day, create a list of tasks you wish to accomplish, ranking them in order of importance. Focus on completing the most critical tasks first and only move on to the next priority once they are completed.

Learn to say no: Recognize that you cannot do everything and that sometimes, saying no is necessary. Decline requests or delegate tasks when they do not align with your priorities or when your plate is already full.

The Art of Focus

Once you have prioritized your tasks, it is crucial to maintain focus and minimize distractions.

Here are three techniques to sharpen your focus and boost productivity:

Limit multitasking: Although multitasking may seem like a productivity booster, it often leads to decreased efficiency and increased errors. Instead, focus on completing one task at a time, fully immersing yourself in the work at hand.

Leverage time blocking: Dedicate specific blocks of time to particular tasks or activities, eliminating distractions during these periods. This technique can help you maintain focus, create a sense of urgency, and promote a healthy work-life balance.

Take breaks: Regular breaks are essential for maintaining mental clarity and focus. Schedule brief pauses throughout your day to rest, recharge, and refresh your mind.

As you embark on your journey toward time management mastery, remember that the power to prioritize and focus is within your grasp. By implementing the strategies and techniques outlined in this chapter, you will unleash your potential for extraordinary productivity and efficiency, propelling yourself toward greatness in your leadership journey. The time is now; seize the moment and make every second count.

Chapter 24

Unleashing the Power Within Embracing Challenges and Cultivating a Growth Mindset

The path to success is paved with challenges, and how we approach them can profoundly affect our personal and professional growth. To unlock our full potential and thrive as leaders, we must adopt a growth mindset – a perspective that views challenges as opportunities for learning and development.

Dr. Carol S. Dweck, a pioneering psychologist, introduced the concept of growth mindset in her groundbreaking book, "Mindset: The New Psychology of Success." A growth mindset empowers us to embrace challenges, persist in the face of setbacks, and see effort as a stepping stone to mastery. In this chapter, we will explore strategies to cultivate a growth mindset and unlock the boundless possibilities that await us.

Rewiring Your Mind for Growth

Developing a growth mindset requires a shift in the way we perceive ourselves, our abilities, and the world around us.

Here are four strategies to rewire your mind for growth:

Embrace failure as a learning opportunity: Recognize that failure is an essential part of the journey toward success. Rather than fearing or avoiding it, view it as a valuable lesson that can help you grow and improve.

Challenge your limiting beliefs: Identify and confront the beliefs that hold you back, such as self-doubt or a fear of taking risks. Replace them with empowering thoughts that reinforce your ability to learn, adapt, and succeed.

Cultivate curiosity: Approach new experiences with curiosity and an eagerness to learn. Embrace the unknown and remain open to exploring new ideas, perspectives, and opportunities.

Practice self-compassion: Be kind to yourself when faced with setbacks or failures. Acknowledge your efforts, and remind yourself that growth is a continuous process that requires patience and persistence.

Transforming Challenges into Opportunities

With a growth mindset firmly in place, you are now equipped to transform challenges into opportunities for growth and success.

Consider these three approaches:

Set achievable, yet ambitious goals: Establish goals that stretch your abilities and encourage personal growth. Break them down into smaller milestones, and celebrate your progress along the way.

Seek constructive feedback: Regularly solicit feedback from trusted colleagues, mentors, or friends. Use this input to refine your skills, adjust your strategies, and fuel your growth.

Surround yourself with growth-minded individuals: Build a network of people who share your passion for learning and personal development. Their support, encouragement, and inspiration will propel you forward on your journey.

As you embark on your quest to cultivate a growth mindset, remember that the power to transform challenges into opportunities lies within you. By embracing this perspective, you will unlock your true potential and emerge as a resilient, adaptable, and unstoppable force in your leadership journey. The world is your oyster; seize every challenge as an opportunity to grow, learn, and thrive.

Chapter 25

The Harmony of Success Fostering Work-Life Balance for a Thriving and Fulfilling Life

In our pursuit of success, we often find ourselves juggling the demands of our professional and personal lives. Striking the right balance between these two realms is essential for fostering well-being, fulfillment, and sustained achievement. As leaders, it is our responsibility not only to prioritize work-life balance for ourselves but also to create a supportive environment that encourages our team members to do the same.

In this chapter, we will explore the importance of work-life balance, discuss strategies for promoting well-being and fulfillment, and provide actionable tips for fostering a healthy balance in your own life and the lives of those you lead.

The Importance of Work-Life Balance

Work-life balance is the delicate equilibrium between our professional obligations and personal commitments, enabling us to thrive in both domains.

Achieving work-life balance is vital for several reasons:

Enhanced well-being: A healthy balance reduces stress and prevents burnout, promoting mental and physical health.

Increased productivity: When we are well-rested and fulfilled in our personal lives, we can bring our best selves to our professional endeavors, leading to increased efficiency and effectiveness.

Improved relationships: Work-life balance allows us to devote quality time to our family, friends, and loved ones, fostering deeper connections and emotional support.

Personal growth: Pursuing interests and passions outside of work enriches our lives and contributes to our overall growth and development.

Strategies for Promoting Work-Life Balance

As leaders, we play a crucial role in cultivating a culture that values work-life balance.

Here are four strategies to encourage well-being and fulfillment among your team members:

Lead by example: Model healthy work-life balance practices, such as taking breaks, setting boundaries, and prioritizing self-care. When you prioritize your own well-being, your team will feel empowered to do the same.

Foster flexibility: Encourage flexible work arrangements, such as remote work or flexible hours, allowing team members to balance their personal and professional responsibilities more effectively.

Encourage time off: Promote the importance of taking time off to rest, recharge, and pursue personal interests. Ensure that your team members feel comfortable taking vacations and unplugging from work.

Recognize and reward balance: Acknowledge and celebrate team members who successfully maintain a healthy work-life balance. This recognition reinforces the value of balance within your organization.

Actionable Tips for Achieving Work-Life Balance

Implementing work-life balance in your own life is equally important.

Consider these tips to promote your well-being and fulfillment:

Set boundaries: Clearly define the boundaries between your work and personal life, and communicate these boundaries to your colleagues and loved ones.

Prioritize self-care: Make time for activities that promote physical, mental, and emotional well-being, such as exercise, meditation, and hobbies.

Develop a support network: Build a network of friends, family, and colleagues who understand the importance of work-life balance and can offer support and encouragement.

Practice mindfulness: Cultivate mindfulness to stay present in each moment, whether at work or in your personal life. This presence allows you to fully engage in and appreciate every aspect of your life.

In conclusion, fostering work-life balance is essential for promoting well-being, fulfillment, and long-term success. By implementing the strategies and tips outlined in this chapter, you will empower yourself and your team members to thrive both personally and professionally. Remember, the journey to work-life balance is an ongoing process; commit to nurturing this harmony for a more fulfilling and successful life.

Chapter 26

The Art of Connection Mastering Active Listening to Deepen Relationships and Enhance Collaboration

In a world inundated with distractions and noise, the ability to truly hear and understand others is a powerful leadership skill. Active listening is more than just hearing the words someone speaks; it is about fully engaging with their message, seeking to understand their perspective, and validating their emotions. By practicing active listening, you can build trust, foster collaboration, and create an environment where everyone feels heard and valued.

In this chapter, we will explore the benefits of active listening, discuss techniques for mastering this essential skill, and provide actionable tips to help you become a more effective communicator and leader.

The Power of Active Listening

Active listening offers numerous benefits for leaders and their teams:

Building trust: When you listen attentively and empathetically, you demonstrate respect and show that you genuinely care about the thoughts and feelings of others, fostering trust and rapport.

Enhancing collaboration: Active listening promotes open communication and the exchange of ideas, leading to more effective teamwork and problem solving.

Preventing misunderstandings: By taking the time to truly understand the messages being communicated, you can minimize misunderstandings, reduce conflict, and make more informed decisions.

Strengthening relationships: Active listening deepens connections and helps you build strong, lasting relationships with team members, colleagues, and clients.

Techniques for Mastering Active Listening

Becoming an active listener requires practice and commitment.

Here are five techniques to help you hone this crucial skill:

Give your full attention: Eliminate distractions, maintain eye contact, and focus solely on the speaker, signaling your interest and engagement.

Be patient: Allow the speaker to finish their thoughts without interrupting. Give them the time and space they need to express themselves fully.

Reflect and paraphrase: Summarize the speaker's main points to ensure understanding and demonstrate that you have been actively engaged in the conversation.

Ask open-ended questions: Encourage further exploration of the topic by asking questions that prompt thoughtful responses and deeper insights.

Show empathy: Validate the speaker's emotions and acknowledge their feelings, creating a supportive and compassionate environment.

Actionable Tips for Practicing Active Listening

To integrate active listening into your daily interactions, consider these tips:

Develop self-awareness: Recognize your own biases, preconceptions, and listening habits that may interfere with your ability to actively listen.

Cultivate a curious mindset: Approach conversations with genuine curiosity, seeking to learn from others and expand your understanding.

Practice mindfulness: Utilize mindfulness techniques, such as deep breathing or meditation, to help you stay present and focused during conversations.

Create a culture of active listening: Encourage active listening within your team and organization by modeling the behavior, providing training, and celebrating examples of effective communication.

Mastering active listening is an invaluable skill for leaders seeking to deepen relationships, foster collaboration, and create a culture where everyone feels heard and valued. By implementing the techniques and tips outlined in this chapter, you will strengthen your communication skills and become a more empathetic, effective leader. Remember, the art of connection begins with truly hearing and understanding others.

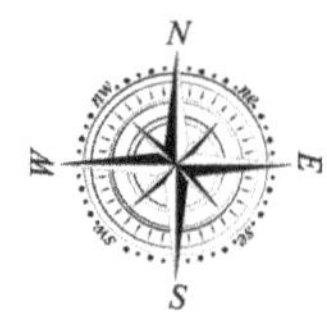

Chapter 27

The Gift of Insight Delivering Constructive Feedback to Empower Growth and Development

Constructive feedback is a vital component of effective leadership, enabling team members to improve, grow, and reach their full potential. By providing thoughtful guidance and support, you not only help individuals develop professionally, but also contribute to the success of your entire team. In this chapter, we will explore the importance of constructive feedback, discuss techniques for delivering it effectively, and offer actionable tips to help you refine your feedback skills.

The Power of Constructive Feedback

Constructive feedback offers numerous benefits for both leaders and their teams:

Fostering growth and development: Feedback helps individuals identify their strengths and weaknesses, offering opportunities for learning and improvement.

Encouraging accountability: Providing feedback promotes personal responsibility, empowering team members to take ownership of their performance and development.

Enhancing team dynamics: Open and honest communication builds trust, encourages collaboration, and fosters a supportive work environment.

Driving performance: Regular feedback motivates team members to continuously improve and strive for excellence.

Techniques for Delivering Constructive Feedback

To deliver constructive feedback effectively, consider the following techniques:

Be specific and objective: Focus on specific behaviors or actions, using clear and objective language to describe the issue at hand.

Offer context: Explain the impact of the behavior on the team, project, or organization to help the individual understand the importance of addressing it.

Balance positive and negative feedback: Acknowledge the individual's strengths and accomplishments, while also discussing areas for improvement.

Be solution-focused: Offer guidance and support to help the individual develop a plan for addressing the issue and achieving their goals.

Deliver feedback promptly: Address issues as they arise, rather than waiting for formal performance reviews, to enable timely learning and growth.

Actionable Tips for Providing Constructive Feedback

To enhance your feedback skills, consider these tips:

Cultivate self-awareness: Recognize your own biases and emotions, ensuring that your feedback is based on objective observations rather than personal feelings.

Practice active listening: Listen carefully to the individual's perspective, demonstrating empathy and understanding as they share their thoughts and concerns.

Create a feedback-friendly culture: Encourage open communication within your team and organization, and model the behavior by seeking feedback on your own performance.

Develop your emotional intelligence: Enhance your ability to recognize, understand, and manage emotions, both in yourself and in others, to deliver feedback more effectively.

The gift of insight through constructive feedback is an essential tool for empowering growth and development in your team members. By implementing the techniques and tips outlined in this chapter, you will become a more effective and supportive leader. Remember, feedback is not about criticism; it is about nurturing potential and guiding individuals on their journey to personal and professional success.

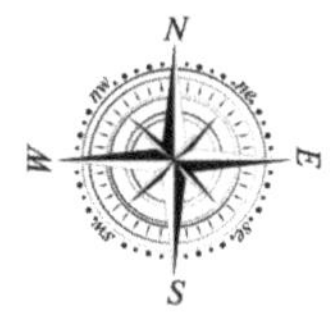

Chapter 28

Fanning the Flames Inspiring Motivation to Fuel Passion and Commitment

The driving force behind success, motivation is the invisible hand that pushes us forward, ignites our passion, and strengthens our commitment. As a leader, one of your essential responsibilities is to inspire and nurture motivation within your team members, empowering them to reach their full potential. In this chapter, we will delve into the role of motivation in leadership, discuss strategies for inspiring motivation, and provide actionable tips to help you invigorate your team.

The Power of Motivation

Motivation is the internal or external drive that compels us to act, learn, and achieve.

It plays a pivotal role in leadership, influencing key factors such as:

Performance: Motivated individuals are more likely to be engaged, focused, and productive, leading to higher performance levels.

Job satisfaction: Employees who feel motivated and passionate about their work often experience greater job satisfaction.

Retention: Motivated team members are more likely to remain loyal and committed to the organization, reducing turnover.

Innovation: When people are motivated, they are more likely to take risks, think creatively, and develop innovative solutions to problems.

Strategies for Inspiring Motivation

To inspire motivation within your team, consider the following strategies:

Set clear goals and expectations: Provide your team with well-defined goals and objectives that align with their skills and interests, creating a sense of purpose and direction.

Offer autonomy and support: Encourage team members to take ownership of their work, providing the freedom to make decisions while also offering guidance and resources as needed.

Recognize and reward achievements: Acknowledge team members' accomplishments, praising their efforts and offering tangible rewards when appropriate.

Foster a growth mindset: Encourage continuous learning and development, emphasizing the importance of embracing challenges and viewing setbacks as opportunities for growth.

Actionable Tips for Energizing Your Team

To further inspire motivation within your team, consider these tips:

Communicate a compelling vision: Share your organization's mission and vision, painting a vivid picture of the future and illustrating how each team member plays a critical role in realizing that vision.

Build strong relationships: Get to know your team members on a personal level, understanding their goals, values, and passions, and use that knowledge to tailor your motivational strategies.

Encourage collaboration: Foster an environment of teamwork and cooperation, where team members feel empowered to share ideas, support one another, and work together to achieve common goals.

Lead by example: Demonstrate your own passion, commitment, and enthusiasm for your work, modeling the behavior and mindset you wish to see in your team.

Inspiring motivation is a vital aspect of effective leadership, enabling your team members to unlock their full potential and contribute meaningfully to your organization's success. By applying the strategies and tips outlined in this chapter, you can fan the flames of motivation, fueling your team's passion and commitment to achieve extraordinary results. Remember, as a leader, you have the power to ignite the spark within each individual, inspiring them to reach new heights and make a lasting impact.

1. Developing a Strong Organizational Culture: Shaping Your Team's Identity
2. Valuing Transparency: Encouraging Openness and Honesty
3. Building Social Capital: Creating and Maintaining Strong Networks
4. Practicing Ethical Decision-Making: Choosing the Right Path
5. Embracing Sustainability: Balancing Profit, People, and Planet
6. Maintaining a Long-Term Perspective: Planning for the Future
7. Cultivating a Sense of Purpose: Aligning Values and Goals
8. Encouraging Autonomy: Giving Team Members Ownership and Control
9. Implementing Strategic Thinking: Planning for Success
10. Acknowledging Mistakes: Learning from Failure
11. Managing Conflict: Navigating Difficult Conversations and Situations

12. Practicing Self-Compassion: Treating Yourself with Kindness and Understanding

13. Investing in Personal Development: Continuously Improving Your Skills

14. Building a Personal Brand: Defining and Communicating Your Unique Value

15. Networking Effectively: Building and Maintaining Strong Relationship

16. Developing Mentorship: Guiding and Supporting Others in Their Growth

17. Celebrating Success: Recognizing and Appreciating Achievements

18. Encouraging Social Responsibility: Contributing to the Greater Good

19. Practicing Mindfulness: Cultivating Presence and Awareness

20. Embracing Vulnerability: Being Open and Authentic with Others

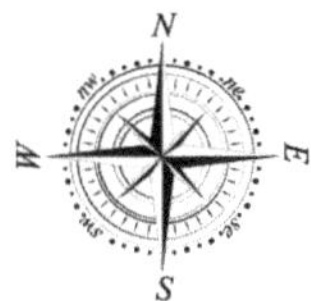

Commentaries

As we journey deeper into this exploration of integrity-driven leadership, we arrive at a pivotal moment in our narrative. This is where the fabric of our discussion evolves; transcending traditional boundaries to embrace a broader, and dialogue that is more inclusive.

The design of this book, intentionally unconventional, mirrors the very essence of integrity itself – dynamic, multifaceted, and boundless. In the first half, we immersed ourselves in the foundational principles of integrity, understanding its profound impact on leadership and personal growth. Now, we pivot to an extraordinary collective journey.

Picture this: a vibrant symposium of the world's most forward-thinking minds. In the pages that follow, you will encounter an assembly of handpicked experts – behavioral scientists, New York Times bestselling authors, NCAA champions, successful entrepreneurs, and more. Each of them is not just a leader in their field but a living testament to the power of integrity.

These individuals have not only achieved remarkable success in their respective arenas; they have done so by steadfastly adhering to the principles of integrity. They lead by example, embodying the virtues we have discussed and demonstrating the tangible impact of integrity in varied and challenging environments.

As you engage with their insights, remember that each voice adds a unique tone to the symphony of integrity-driven leadership. From the analytical rigor of behavioral scientists to the passionate narratives of NCAA champions, and the strategic acumen of successful entrepreneurs, this is a tapestry woven from diverse strands of excellence.

This section of the book is more than just a compilation of expert opinions. It is an invitation to a larger conversation, a call to join a community of thought leaders who are redefining success and leadership through the lens of integrity. As Simon Sinek often emphasizes, true leadership is about creating a vision that inspires others to join you on a journey – a journey not just towards individual success, but also towards a more ethical, empathetic, and united world.

In embracing these narratives, you are not just reading another chapter; you are stepping into a realm of endless possibilities. Here, the concept of integrity is not just discussed; it is brought to life through stories, experiences, and wisdom that transcend the written word.

So, as you turn these pages, prepare to be inspired, challenged, and transformed. Welcome to the heart of our book, where the principles of integrity meet the real world – a world where leadership is not just about the position you hold, but also about the stand you take.

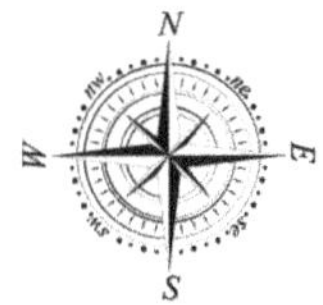

Ava V Manuel on Integrity

The Foundation for Wholeness, Fulfillment, and Success

Have you ever found yourself overworking, stressing out, unfulfilled, self-loathing, or unworthy?

When we look closely into anything that produces these feelings, we will find a breach in our integrity.

Without being grounded in what is in integrity for us and making it a standard for our decisions and actions, we are pulled in different directions - distracted by other people's opinions and demands. We become what the Bible describes as "double-minded, unstable, and tossed to and fro."

I was there. For years, I worked hard to maintain a reputation as a person of integrity. My radical change began when I understood this powerful distinction: reputation is not equal to integrity. Reputation is how others perceive you. Integrity is how you perceive yourself.

Integrity starts from within by being aware of your values and grounded in your truth. It takes form when you align and act consistently with your truth in everything you say, even to yourself alone and in everything you do. When we take action through the lenses of our values, being in integrity is our natural self-expression.

When challenges cause us to derail from our integrity: being in fear of what others would think and what others will say, wanting to look good or be right, or being determined to create certain results, realize that it always costs us more to be out of integrity than to be in integrity.

My great mentor Nick Berar taught me a straightforward truth that reveals when we are out of integrity somewhere in our life. "Anytime anything is not working, it's an integrity issue."

Understanding this, whenever I find something that is not working for me, *I practice three steps:*

First, I take the time to go back to the basics of what is true by allowing myself to be curious – without judgment. I remove myself from any attachment to what's happening, and I put myself into neutral observation. Just matter-of-factly, looking at whatever findings as data and feedback.

Getting into neutral is an important entry point into exploration and discovery. It creates a safe space where your guards go down, your resistances dissipate, your blocks give way, and your conscious and subconscious faculties become willing to discover and see things with honest clarity.

Second, I acknowledge and clear with myself any breakdown in my integrity that I find where I have acted incongruently with my values and with what is truly important to me.

The truth is, our inner self knows and holds it against us when we ignore our inner voice and betray ourselves or when we do not do what we say we will do, even to ourselves. Over time, it shows up as resistance, avoidance, procrastination, lack of confidence, difficulty with trusting and making decisions, and self-hatred.

So, I forgive myself, and others if need be. I clean up anything I find that I have secretly held against myself with surrender and forgiveness. I start with a clean slate: without offense, without self-beat up, without self-hatred, and with welcoming and eventually, with unconditional acceptance.

"Forgiveness is giving up the hope that the past could have been any different. It's accepting the past for what it was, and using this moment and this time to help yourself move forward."

– Oprah Winfrey

When you're in a place where there's nothing you want to change, nothing you don't like, nothing you feel bad about or wish were different, you'll find that where you are right now is where your Divine Higher Power knew you would be all along. There is no misalignment, no regret, no burden, no effort, no sacrifice, no discomfort, no fault, no guilt, no blame, and no shame.

This state of radical acceptance and unconditional love is the way of being, and it is not just a concept that experientially exists when we are authentic and walking in integrity. It opens up possibilities to repair, rebuild, restore, and create, leading us perfectly to my next step.

Third, *I acknowledge and clean up any breach of integrity I created with those affected by my incongruence.* I own up to where I have allowed pressure or fear or wanting to please others or gain something to derail my decision-making in a way that affected them.

At the end of it, my ultimate goal is to always get back to integrity. It is costly - in time, energy, relationships, resources, finances, and opportunities to not be in integrity.

Integrity produces workability and leads to honest solutions, expansion of one's capacity, creativity, and clarity. Therefore, whatever it takes and however much it costs, it is always worth returning to integrity.

Continuing to align with one's integrity, however, is a life-long ongoing journey. So, while you are at it, find ways to make it fun, and be sure to enjoy the journey.

Ben Hummell, LPC, LMFT on Integrity

Years ago, while I was trying to settle on an image for my brand logo, I was consistently drawn back to one of the most iconic drawings from recent human history, Leonardo DaVinci's Vitruvian man. If you're a live human being and reading this, chances are that you've seen this image of a man with two sets of outstretched arms and legs within a circle and a square.

DaVinci drew this impactful image of a human based on the ideas of the Roman architect Vitruvius who saw the human body as the principal source of proportion and beauty. He proposed the idea that all of the proportions of the natural universe are represented and reflected in the basic design of a human. The man is depicted inside of a circle representing the cosmos and the natural balance of things, and then the circle intersects with a square, representing the earth and the material world. The power and import of this image is the representation of balance, where both energies, cosmic and material are represented and functioning TOGETHER. This archetypal symbol depicts the integrity of the foundational and undivided essence of a human being.

This means that the fullest state of an individual is one who is no longer divided within themselves, just like a whole number is one that is not divided into fractions. This indivisibility or integrity can take a bit of work for us to attain. But by using the correct tools and practices throughout our life, along with developing a deeper sense of self-awareness and introspection, we can learn to think, speak, act, express, and create from a unity of the cosmic and the material world. When we do, our values, principles, character, and connection to existence all come together as an integrated whole that serves to bring us a sense of meaning, purpose, and fulfillment.

So true integrity is about the cosmic and the personal being used together, as a unified field of expression. One without the other when we're creating or expressing something is only a halfmeasure. The act of finding our calling and presenting our gifts to the world is to gather both of the aspects of our nature together into our actions and offerings, and into our relationships and businesses.

As we move into our personal projects and endeavors, it is vital to take this balance of cosmic and personal into all that we do, so that we're moving with the flow of our connection with existence instead of against it. And it is important to know that the deepest part of ourselves IS existence. And while many of us don't live with this fact as a day-to-day experience, those who do can be said to be living with integrity because they are aligned with the qualities of existence, such as creativity, potential, and possibility as well as their individual values and principles.

Another aspect that I put into my logo was a compass, representing life direction. Many of us struggle with this basic issue of not having a purposeful direction in life, and here is where our personal integrity can become quite thin and challenged. Without a governing sense of direction in our lives, we tend to waste a lot of time wandering from one project to another without gaining much traction toward our life goals. Finding our own life direction starts at the foundation of where our cosmic and material selves meet. There is a blueprint and map already there for our life journey, and we need to develop the skill to look and listen very deeply for its guidance and instruction.

Integrity in a person can also be described as a wholeness of character. The word character comes from the Greek word *kharakter*, which is an engraving tool. The metaphor, then is that of a mark or imprint on our soul as we grow, deepen, and develop throughout our life. It's been said that if you want a good representation of someone's character, look to the person they are and the actions they take when no one is looking. So, developing a stable, consistent, and reliable character is part of the purpose of our life experience, bringing us into a state of natural wholeness, unity, and balance. These qualities become our personal (character) traits, and these traits reflect the integrity of ourselves in balance with existence.

My personal vision and work, The Genius Way® is about empowering others to find and acknowledge their Genius as an everyday experience, and to express their lives from that part of their identity. An aspect of that work is to bring others' awareness to how their values, and principles can align with their creative vision and expression.

Individual Genius is existence's creative expression through us. And each one of us has this quality at our core. The gifts we came here to share with the world are contained in our Genius DNA, the place where we are still connected inextricably with existence. When we express from there, the cosmic and the personal within us are integrated, and our expression is deep, potent, and transformative both for ourselves and the world we live in. We can see ourselves as the Vitruvian man, centered in both existence and individuality, aware, connected, and alive with purpose.

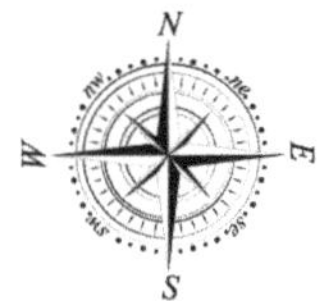

Bill Walsh on Integrity

As I reflect on my decades-long journey working with entrepreneurs from all walks of life, one thing stands out as the bedrock of lasting success: integrity. Throughout my career, I have seen countless examples of individuals who have soared to great heights, not only in business but also in life, because of their unwavering commitment to integrity. In this chapter, I will delve into the concept of integrity, share my insights on why it is essential, and outline how you can foster this invaluable trait in your personal and professional life.

Integrity, in its simplest form, is the quality of being honest, reliable, and upholding strong moral principles. It is the foundation upon which trust is built, and it is no secret that trust is the lifeblood of any successful relationship—be it personal or professional. As a business leader, your integrity is constantly under scrutiny. Stakeholders, employees, and clients are all watching your actions, and your commitment to integrity can make or break your reputation.

When I think about the entrepreneurs who have made a lasting impression on me, it's not their intelligence, skillset, or even charisma that comes to mind; it's their unwavering commitment to integrity. These individuals have the courage to do the right thing, even when it is difficult or unpopular. They honor their promises, stand by their word, and treat others with respect.

As a leader, your integrity sets the tone for your entire organization. When you demonstrate integrity in your actions and decisions, you inspire others to do the same. This creates a culture of trust and accountability, where people feel empowered to take responsibility for their actions and work together towards a common goal.

Great leaders understand that integrity is not a one-time act; it is a lifelong commitment that must be nurtured and reinforced every day. Embodying integrity means embracing humility, staying true to your values, and always striving to improve. It means facing challenges with courage and grace, even when the path ahead is uncertain.

In the end, it is our integrity that will define us. When the dust settles and our accomplishments fade into the annals of history, our character will endure. As you embark on your entrepreneurial journey, I encourage you to make integrity the cornerstone of your success. Be the leader who inspires trust, who models ethical behavior, and who leaves a legacy of honor and commitment.

Remember, your success is not only measured by the wealth you amass or the accolades you receive but also by the lives you touch and the positive impact you make on the world. Let integrity be your guiding star and you will not only achieve greatness in business but also in life.

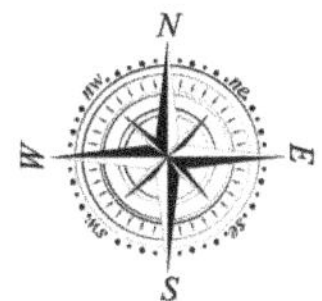

Carissa Johnsen on Integrity

Spiritual Grit for High Powered Integrity Driven Leadership

Integrity is the basis of personal character. It requires an unwavering commitment to truth even when you are internal or external world appears to be crumbling. It stands as the cornerstone upon which people and empires rise and fall. Integrity, in the sacred tapestry of leadership, is not just a word; it is a perpetual invitation. For deeper self-understanding, authentic expression, compassionate connection, and a call to passionate love in action, which is true power.

This power is found in leaders who embody an unapologetic dedication to spiritual principles that can reshape the very fabric of our society. These qualities are cultivated from within and stem from encountering situations in which a leader has to confront their shadow. What starts as a whisper from God/Source, can turn into an entire collapse of existence, forcing the leader to completely dismantle their identity, values, belief systems, and behavior and then rebuild. This is the journey from trauma to truth, from head to heart, and from the love of power to the power of love. This is the dreaded, and yet highly coveted opportunity to develop Spiritual Grit.

Grit, in the realm of leadership, is the backbone of integrity, the unshakable resolve to stay true to our higher selves, no matter what is on the line. The reason I can speak so intensely about this topic is that I have lived it. Through experiencing a shattering of my reality, I had to call upon a power greater than me. To tap into a source that far exceeded my humanness. This initiation was painful in that it cracked me open to immense suffering and yet instilled in me a truth that could never be taught from a book or teacher--- its necessity was experiential. This embodied wisdom has allowed me to step into the fierce realm of integrity-driven leadership or spirit-led leadership, with an unwavering conviction of who I am, and what I stand for, and to trust divine intelligence.

In 2021, I was living out the dream. On paper, everything appeared exceptional. I had a beautiful penthouse in San Diego. I just leased a brand new Range Rover and adopted an adorable Shih Tzu. I had a full roster of clients, and incredibly gifted team members, launching successful retreats and bringing in consistent four or 5-figure cash months. This was the life I worked so hard to build and what I thought I always wanted. Except it was not.

Sure, I had designer clothes, a social media influence, and 100,000 dollars in the bank. Yet, I could barely get out of bed. Riddled with anxiety, overwhelmed with messages from clients, and a body that was in pain due to gut and hormonal issues, I knew I was hitting rock bottom. On one of my worst days, I nearly crawled to my bathroom floor, with swollen eyes and I stood up. I looked at myself in the mirror and realized that I did not know who Carissa was. Outside of the image I manufactured, I felt unsafe no matter how much money I had. I felt insignificant no matter how many followers. I felt unwell and yearning for a connection to something other than business. I lacked wholeness, health, intimacy, and safety. I was unhappy and I was seeking the illusion of societal standard of success, at all costs. I wanted to live an authentic life and yet I was worried about what would happen if I continued to go in this direction.

As soon as I realized that I was outsourcing my power to materialism, vanity metrics, and hierarchies, I knew that my entire life needed to change. I sensed that whatever I was embarking on would not be easy, but I lacked awareness of how much it would test my strength. I knew that I was going to need to choose to lean into this path every single day.

For the next two years, I consciously deconstructed myself to get to the core of my wounding, which was the belief that I was not enough. I witnessed how the lies were infused in everything I created for myself. I then watched it all fall away. What remained was my truest essence. It was I and I was enough regardless of how much money I had, what kind of clothes I wore or the car I drove. I loved myself.

As you can tell, I made it to the other side. One of the greatest lessons I learned was that it is not merely the ability to endure hardships, but a profound belief in a higher purpose, a cosmic plan that transcends the challenges of the present moment. I believe that human potentiality is discovered when we are asked to go far beyond what we think we are capable of. Leaders who can go more deeply inward and reach higher for spiritual guidance can end the war they are fighting within themselves and develop an ineffable courage that allows them to become victorious no matter what they go through.

Life teachings like this, remind us of our divinity and the eternal nature of the soul. Grit, one of the main ingredients in the alchemical formula, transmutes adversity, cultivates resilience, and turns an ordinary individual into an extraordinary leader. Every triumph becomes a testament to the power of grit, unwavering faith, and the human spirit.

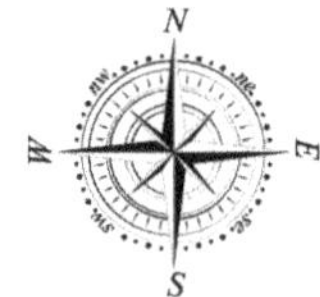

Catherine King, on Integrity

Headed North?

Where are you headed? Life often seems linear in its direction but sometimes we find ourselves without an *end* game. Directionless existence is void of meaning. So, let's start at the beginning: *purpose.*

We were born to reproduce. Returning to the words of the ancient "good book", in the very first chapter, we receive a twofold instruction in Genesis 1: 28 to "be fruitful and multiply." That is the first thing we are told to do and that is not simply an instruction to procreate! Rather, we are called to perpetuate values reflective of the divine nature in every context of our lives: family, friends, community, work, nation, and indeed, our world!

The word "fruitful" refers to meaningful productivity and "multiply" means to increase. That is exactly what *legacy* is – the fruitfulness and increase in our lives passed on to future generations. Yet, it is far more than the accumulation of assets; rather it is a values-based empowerment of inheritance.

Peter Strople writes: "Legacy is not leaving something for people. It's leaving something *in* people." Legacy represents lasting values that impact others throughout our lives, while integrity speaks to the consistent alignment of our values with our actions. *Together,* these qualities define an individual's character and their life's imprint on others. One without the other produces little of lasting consequence.

Consider an American classroom. It will be clear the type of home a child comes from those with strong values and integrity – and those without. "Jennifer" has parents, who consistently guide her in ways of character and wisdom, and she is known for her kindness and opportunities abound. Alternatively,

"Samuel" is from a divided home lacking integrity and counsel, and he regularly suffers harsh consequences from poor choices. The difference in the future for these children is stark in contrast and reflective of what is (or is not) being produced in these respective homes. What separates them? Integrity.

Integrity is a powerful word in a world where talk is often cheap!

Napoleon Hill once said, "Integrity is the foundation upon which *all* other values are built."

Integrity at its root means "whole" or "complete" and represents the consistent *integration* of values with action. Values such as compassion, honesty, generosity, and excellence consistently applied over time not only provide a moral compass for choices in life, but they also carry the weight of trust and authenticity. By imparting values grounded in character, we create a ripple effect of positive change. Just as a seed can grow into a fruitful tree, the reproduction of values rooted in integrity shapes future generations. Oprah writes, "When you align your actions with your values, you will find yourself heading toward your true north." The "Jennifers" and "Samuels" of our world are separated largely by the depth of integrity experienced in their homes.

Marketplace leadership demands no less. Dwight Eisenhower confirmed this saying, "The supreme quality for leadership is unquestionably integrity. Without it, no real success is possible..." Workplace impact requires values applied daily to find the "true north" in business.

Integrity and legacy are interconnected like a moral compass guiding our lives. If we view Integrity as the needle of our moral compass, Legacy then becomes the "true North" in our journey. Is your "integrity compass" dialed north? In this framework, the legacy we leave and the integrity we uphold become the *true measure of our success.* A legacy built on integrity – at home or work - holds immeasurable value and impact on our future as individuals and in the community.

So, are you headed north?

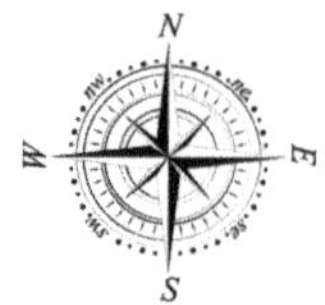

Christina Rendon on Integrity

Embodied Integrity
The Power of Authentic Alignment
Christina Rendon

In the intricate journey of personal evolution, integrity illuminates a path to experiencing alignment within ourselves and throughout our lives. It serves as a compass, guiding us through the labyrinth of self-discovery, towards the intersection of our actions and deeper beliefs or connection to life. Integrity entails embracing our values and consistently acting in a way that aligns with our standards in life.

In our ever-evolving life, opportunities to progress or grow consistently arise. Integrity plays a vital role in the transformation of our mental and emotional well-being. It also possesses the potential to nurture our overall sense of wellness and amplify our capacity to navigate the diverse aspects of our lives.

The construct of integrity comprises both an inner and an outer dimension. Our inner reality encompasses various aspects, from our individual perspectives and preferences to our very way of being, our self-awareness, and the ebbs and flows of our emotions. When this inner reality aligns or is in congruence with our external world, we experience a greater sense of wholeness and embody our authentic potential. Through cultivating this alignment across the various dimensions of our lives, we can elevate our life's quality, empower our ability to shape the life we aspire to, and ultimately feel deeply connected in life.

Integrity is the sincere dedication to our values and vision, not just towards others or in life, but in some aspects, even more crucially towards ourselves.

By embracing integrity, we engage in a dance where authenticity merges with the intentional creation of our lives.

The interconnectedness between integrity and mental well-being is profound. Upholding our values through actions often cultivates inner harmony and the ability to access more intentional energy in how we engage with life. Conversely, acting in discordance with our principles can lead to a sense of disconnection and less of an ability to consciously influence the unfolding of our lives. When we feel disconnected from our core selves, integrity acts as a bridge, bridging the gap between our inner essence and outward choices. Similarly, if we perceive a distance from our aspirations for growth, integrity guides us toward embodying our renewed self.

The path toward embracing integrity is realized by the understanding that the gap between who we are and who we strive to become can be bridged. We initiate true transformation by taking intentional steps—assessing areas where we fall short of integrity within and without, committing to authentic living, and creating congruence with our true selves. As we elevate our energy and resonance, we align ourselves with a reality that resonates with our genuine power and joy.

In essence, your journey toward integrity beautifully mirrors the transformative potential each of us holds within. Integrity can bridge the gap between who we are and who we aspire to be. It also bridges the divide between individual transformation and how we contribute to life. Through embracing integrity, we can feel more of a sense of wholeness, authenticity, and ability to guide the creation of our lives.

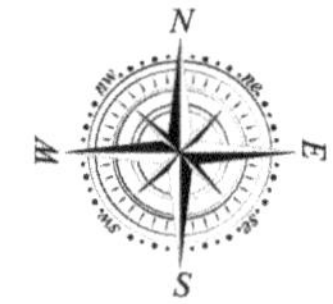

Craig Bruce on Integrity

The Journey to Unreasonable Excellence

It was all fine until it was not.

After years of global management consulting and constant travel, I reached a breaking point. I was exhausted, struggling with my health, and feeling disconnected from myself and others. It was during a period of forced bed rest that I had my big "aha" moment.

As I lay there, working from my bed, I realized I had neglected my well-being and key relationships for far too long. I saw the toll it had taken on me physically, mentally, and emotionally. It was at that moment that I made a firm decision to change my lifestyle and take control of my health and fulfillment.

In pursuing a life of boundless possibilities and unwavering excellence, I discovered that staying true to my core values, establishing a foundation grounded in integrity and embracing unreasonableness as my driving force would allow me to unlock my potential to live limitlessly.

In this pursuit of excellence, my values served as guiding lights. Connection to Source, Health and Wellness, Long-term Relationships, Diversity and Inclusion define who I am at my core. They acted as compasses, directing my choices and actions while forming the moral and ethical foundation upon which I built my life.

When I got clear and intentional about my values, I made decisions aligned with my authentic self. These values served as filters, guiding me toward opportunities aligned with my purpose and helping me navigate challenges with integrity and authenticity.

Integrity, the essence of moral character, propelled me toward a life of authenticity and trust. Living in integrity became my unwavering commitment to align my actions with my values, keeping my word, and honoring my responsibilities. It enabled me to nurture connections that are more genuine, cultivate greater trust, and empowered me to build a life based on unwavering principles. When I embodied integrity, I created a life rooted in truth and authenticity, leading to a sense of purpose and fulfillment.

To reach new heights of achievement, I embraced unreasonableness within integrity. Unreasonableness is the audacious act of defying conventional wisdom, challenging limits, and daring to dream beyond what was deemed possible. It involved thinking big, taking calculated risks, and pursuing passions relentlessly.

Unreasonableness was not about reckless abandon. It was a deliberate choice to tap into my limitless potential and break free from self-imposed limitations. It demanded the courage to persist in adversity and embrace innovative solutions to overcome challenges.

The harmonious integration of my values, integrity and unreasonableness became a powerful catalyst for a life of possibility and excellence. Living with unwavering integrity ensured that my actions aligned with my core values. Embracing unreasonableness empowered me to challenge boundaries, dream big and persevere through obstacles to realize the extraordinary.

My transformative journey exemplifies the extraordinary power of unwavering values, integrity, and unreasonableness. Integrating these elements into my life, has unlocked the door to a world of limitless possibilities.

Today, I embrace my values, live with unwavering integrity, and unleash the power of unreasonableness to create a life that knows no bounds and invite others to embrace this incredible journey.

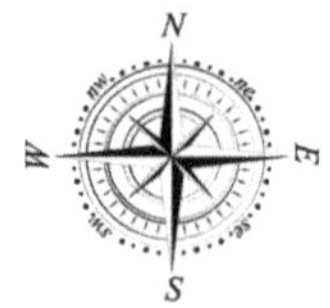

Dagmar Fleming on Integrity

The Athena Circle: A Tale of Integrity and Authentic Leadership

"In diversity, there is beauty, and there is strength."

– Maya Angelou

In the realm of leadership, where principles are tested and decisions bear significant weight, integrity serves as our North Star. What does it truly mean to lead with integrity? In my experience, integrity-driven leadership is not just a buzzword but also a profound commitment to fundamental values that shape our character as leaders. In fact, integrity and authenticity are critically intertwined values that should co-exist side by side.

When I established The Athena Circle as a community for women visionaries seeking lives filled with passion, purpose, and prosperity, little did I foresee that the values we chose to embrace would soon face a significant integrity challenge.

Yet, one day, the true strength of our dedication to these principles would face the ultimate test.

The Athena Circle was founded on the principles of individual sovereignty and respect for diverse expressions – racial, cultural, societal, gender-related, political, or sexual orientation. Inclusivity and authenticity have always been at the heart of our community.

We – the Athenas - recognize that our collective strength thrives on embracing differing perspectives. This openness led us to welcome a transgender woman into our community. Most members embraced her with welcoming hearts, appreciating her unique journey as an addition to our rich tapestry.

However, amid this celebration of diversity, we faced adversity when one member vehemently opposed this inclusion, resorting to verbal abuse. This member demanded the removal of the transgender woman, going as far as criticizing my leadership skills and questioning the organization for allegedly devaluing women. It was a moment that tested our commitment to tolerance of views and authenticity.

In response to this divisive situation, we gathered as a community to voice our concerns and perspectives. Grounded in our ethics of respecting opposing viewpoints, we genuinely valued each member's opinion, understanding that these differences could foster growth and deeper understanding. Regrettably, we found it necessary to request the member who did not align with these beliefs to leave our community. While we respected her right to her own opinion, we stood strong in our inclusivity and tolerance values.

This challenging experience ultimately forged stronger bonds among us, reaffirming that the community we have cultivated is a safe haven for all to express their individuality freely, without fear of judgment or prejudice from others. This challenging episode served as a poignant reminder that integrity-driven leadership means holding true to our ethical principles, even when faced with resistance. Embracing different perspectives and standing firm in our convictions can be challenging at times but is ultimately the path to authentic leadership.

In the end, our experience during this arduous period reinforced the importance of standing up for what we believe in and preserving the integrity of our community, even when faced with adversity. It was a true test of our determination to respect different perspectives, and we emerged from it more united and resolute than ever before.

Authenticity is a cornerstone of an integrity-driven leadership paradigm. Leaders embrace diverse standpoints and expressions, understanding that true wisdom often emerges from unexpected sources. When you encourage open dialogue and inclusivity, you create spaces where individuals feel safe to express their true selves and thus become a catalyst for creativity and progress. Eleanor Roosevelt wisely said, "The purpose of life, after all, is to live it, to taste experience to the utmost, to reach out eagerly and without fear for newer and richer experiences." What fresh perspectives or experiences can you embrace to enrich your life, and in turn, inspire those you lead?

Authentic leadership requires resilience and steadfast dedication to our guiding principles. It is not just about adhering to those core values but embodying them even when they are tested. The Athena Circle stands as a testament to the power of staying true to these ideals in the face of challenges. Our journey through this testing chapter reaffirmed that our commitment to respecting differing viewpoints is not just a slogan but also a living reality. It is a commitment we uphold with resolute resolve, demonstrating that true integrity-driven leadership is not only about the values we profess but also the values we live. What values define you?

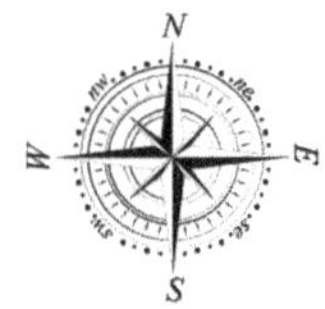

Dan Armstrong on Integrity

Be Aware of Your Presence in the Lives of Other People

How often have you been the recipient of a drive-through freebie?

You know – the guy in front of you paid your tab before you moved forward to collect your food. Maybe that has never happened to you – it has to me! Moreover, I believe the reason is very clear and easy to understand. I have sown where I knew I could not reap. I have given up real cash, real effort, and genuine affection into the lives of those who have nothing to return or are not required to do so.

Integrity for me starts with being aware of MY presence in the lives of OTHER people.

What does that mean?

A brief story may help. I was walking through Baltimore, Maryland, with my children. A beggar approached, asking for money. I reached into my pocket and pulled out two dollars. Once the stranger accepted the gift, he looked up and said, "Thank you."

A man sitting on a park bench nearby commented aloud, "Should you give money to someone who might spend it on drugs or booze?" His commentary was filled with judgment. I ignored the urge to react but used the opportunity to respond, to instruct my children. I said, "Hey guys, I would rather be judged for giving to the wrong person than be judged for not giving at all." I said it loud enough for the guy on the bench to hear me.

I added to the life lesson. I told my daughters to LISTEN to the still, small voice of God within them to discern IF and WHEN to give. There are times that the whisper will tell you NO. Nevertheless, in my life, the YES has often been the answer. Serve others without expectation of recompense.

Being aware of YOUR presence in the lives of OTHER people is not easy in a world of egos, including our own!

Tunnel vision is a disease that puts us at a huge disadvantage when it comes to being aware. You are not the only living being on the planet. We share this globe with billions of people.

A hundred years ago, another population of busy self-serving lives existed who are no longer here. What did they leave behind? One hundred years from now, perhaps the question will be asked, "What did YOU leave behind?"

The basics are so simple, so subtle, and so often slip by without notice. I am asking you to pause, to ponder – Are you aware of your presence in the lives of other people? Are you walking by opportunities to serve another?

If so, why? Why would you give up the greatest blessing and the greatest return on investment of all time by living in a narrow world perspective?

ACTION is your seed, and THIS moment in time is the SOIL of your gift. Do not worry about the receiver; only concern yourself with the gift – the gift of your heart. Your awareness of who YOU ARE and CAN BE in the life of a hurting soul can be your greatest reward. BE aware of YOUR presence.

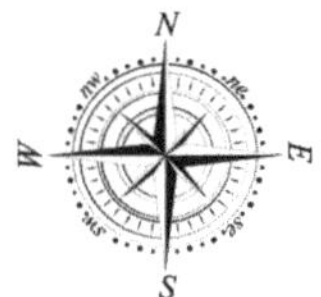

Dannella Burnett on Integrity

Walking the Walk on the Stage

In my experience as an Event Producer and Speaker Strategist, I have had the absolute privilege to work alongside some of the best in the coaching and speaking industry and then, I have seen some of the worst behavior as well. Fortunately, for the most part positive usually outweighs the negative and throughout my journey, I've come to realize that integrity isn't just some fancy buzzword; it's the very essence of who we are and how we impact others.

Integrity, in its simplest form, means walking the talk and staying true to our values. It is about being honest, ethical, and genuine in everything we do. As speakers and experts, integrity should serve as our guiding compass, directing our actions and shaping our character. The rock-solid foundation allows us to establish ourselves as trusted authorities in our respective fields.

For me, integrity starts with delivering on our promises. Our audience and our clients rely on us to provide them with valuable insights, practical advice, and strategies they can implement. By honoring our commitments and delivering what we say we will, we show our genuine dedication to their growth and success. Integrity means we do not exaggerate our abilities or make false claims about our expertise. Instead, we stay grounded in reality, focusing on what we genuinely know and can genuinely offer. Not only is this the right thing to do, but it is in our best interest as well. Audiences are smart and can generally sense whether a speaker is sharing authentically and with a degree of transparency.

We need to be true to ourselves and our audience, sharing our knowledge, experiences, and perspectives openly and honestly. When we reveal our own journeys, including both the highs and lows, we create a real and authentic connection with our listeners. It is through transparency that trust is built, and trust is the bedrock of effective coaching. When our audience sees us as genuine and sincere, they are more likely to engage, learn, and apply the insights we provide. As speakers, we have the incredible honor and responsibility of sharing our stories, and we must take that seriously, knowing the impact our words can have on others.

Moreover, integrity demands that we respect the confidentiality of our clients. As coaches, we are entrusted with sensitive information and personal stories. It is essential that we treat their privacy with the utmost care, maintaining strict confidentiality in all our interactions. Respecting confidentiality creates a safe space where individuals can share their challenges and vulnerabilities. It fosters an environment conducive to growth, empowering clients to fully open up, knowing that their privacy is protected. It is a fine line when sharing about successes and failures is part of connecting and knowing when it crosses the line to oversharing or gossip. I know that I have not always been perfect in finding that line and I have seen hurt I have caused and hurt I have felt being on the other side of that. When we fall short, the path of integrity and back to integrity is owned, repairing and doing better for the future.

We have probably all heard the saying, that character is doing the right thing when no one is looking. It is also doing the right thing when all eyes are on you. I do not know anyone that nails this 100% of the time, but I think we can easily see those that use a strong degree of integrity as their guide.

Finally, as experts, being in integrity calls for our continuous personal and professional development. As speakers and experts, we have a responsibility to stay up-to-date with the latest research, trends, and best practices in our fields. By constantly expanding our knowledge and refining our skills, we uphold the level and status of experts. This commitment to growth not only enhances our own knowledge and abilities but also ensures that we provide the most accurate, relevant, and impactful guidance to our audience and clients.

In conclusion, integrity is the heartbeat of our success as speakers and experts in the coaching industry. It is about delivering on our promises, being transparent and authentic, respecting confidentiality, handling conflicts of interest with care, and committing to continuous development. By embracing integrity, we build trust, forge meaningful connections, and make a profound and lasting positive impact on the lives of those we serve. So, let integrity be the guiding light that illuminates our path as coaches, propelling us towards greater heights of excellence and influence.

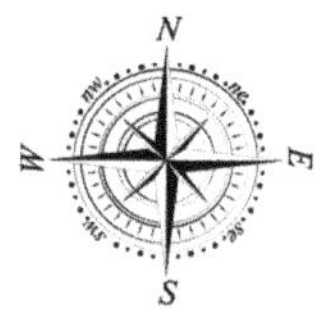

Dawna Campbell on Integrity
The Power of Your Word:
The Key to Living in Integrity

Integrity is a powerful quality that reverberates in every facet of our personal and professional lives, shaping us into the person we aspire to be. This indispensable quality is the foundation to inspire trust, respect, and honesty, forming deep connections with others. Growing up, I observed my father demonstrate the importance of living in integrity every day.

My father was a simple, but yet hardworking man, who lived his life by a code of honor. Watching him closely, he never compromised his principles or values for personal gain and always remained true to his word. "Your word is your bond" I recall my father saying one morning when I was a little girl. "Everything you do can be done with a handshake." Now, my father was few on words, but when he spoke, there was great meaning. Those few words he said to me had a lasting and profound impact. Here are some of the greatest lessons I have learned from his words on integrity.

First and foremost, we must have a desire to live our lives with integrity. Having a strong sense of purpose and a clear set of values is at the crux that guides our behavior. Living with integrity requires a willingness to be held accountable for our decisions and being consistent with our actions, even when it is difficult or uncomfortable. As leaders, the desire to live with integrity must be grounded in a deep sense of personal conviction and a belief that doing the right thing is the only option.

Second, having guidance and support from others is necessary for continued integrity and growth. This can come in many forms, such as mentorship, coaching, or simply having an honest and authentic conversation with some-one. Being open, receptive to feedback, and willing to learn from mistakes, we must strive to be transparent in our interactions. Without integrity, relation-ships become superficial, shallow, and devoid of meaning.

Last, living with integrity can have a remarkable impact on ourselves and those around us. The ripple effect of integrity is both powerful and transfor-mative, drawing others to us and motivating them to do the right thing. Integ-rity is a lifelong pursuit and is not always easy. Sometimes people are more concerned with their own interests and personal gain, such as instances of fraud, corruption, and unethical behavior. As heart-centered leaders, integrity brings opportunities to hold ourselves to the same standards that we expect from others.

The power of your word is truly the key to living in integrity. It is a valuable quality that guides behavior in all aspects of our lives, requiring a desire for personal growth, support, commitment, and a willingness to transform the world around us. By keeping our word and living with integrity, we become powerful agents of change, inspiring those around us to do the same and making a lasting impact on the world we live in.

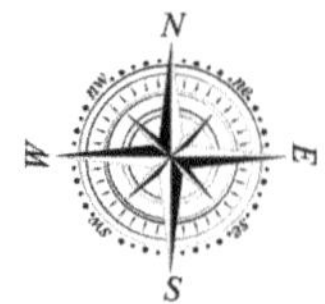

Doria Cordova on Integrity

"Integrity is the essence of everything successful..."
– Buckminster Fuller.

I remember when I first heard this word being repeatedly used by Werner Erhard, the founder of EST, which later evolved into Landmark Education, known as one the pioneer trainings of the human potential movement. I thought that he was speaking about being honest... When I attended a one-day training in which he spoke about the subject, I (along with tens of thousands) discovered a much deeper meaning of what integrity meant.

After 46 years of working on self-mastery––since I first heard Buckminster Fuller speak in 1977––Bucky Fuller's definition, "that which holds its own shape", is now much more congruent with my experience of life.

"Bucky" (as he preferred to be called) was not only a visionary, he was a thinker, an inventor, a "human experiment" as he liked to refer to himself, he was also an architect, and he would discuss integrity from a holistic and systemic perspective.

The dictionary describes integrity as "the quality of being honest and having strong moral principles; moral uprightness." Moreover, a secondary description: "the state of being whole and undivided."

Interestingly though, now people are giving the word their own definition.

Have you ever heard someone say: "S/he is out of integrity..." when they are just not agreeing with their point of view?

Let me offer you my perspective…

Integrity is a very personal experience. People can be very sensitive and very offended if you question their integrity. In the old days, there used to be public feuds over an attack on someone's integrity.

Integrity is important in everyone's life because if you are a highly integrous person, you will be admired, respected, and sought-after by many. It is even more important because YOU are watching your own actions!

If a part of you judges you for doing things that are not congruent with that which you find honorable or respectful, you will unconsciously punish yourself. Your "deservability", your level of abundance, and your success will be highly affected by this lack of self-respect.

In my 44-plus years of being around entrepreneurial, experiential, transformational trainings globally――and personal coaching, mentoring, and supporting many in having the life of their dreams――I have had front-row seating to watching what human beings do when they feel even out of integrity with themselves and others…

Now, of course, we are speaking of good people. I am not speaking of dishonest people who make it a habit to abuse the trust of others, and in the extreme, con artists. I am speaking of good people in general. As a side note, those who make it a habit of being dishonest, leave a trail of dissatisfied clients, customers, suppliers, and even family members.

It is clear that they have no idea what being an integrous human being means. Moreover, I have to say, I have seen cases where there was a reckoning――and awakening―― where they have gone back and redeemed themselves and made things right. They did a "Ho'oponopono in action", which repaired the situation, and even their reputations. It is never too late to be an honest person!

To return to the point: integrity is a very personal experience. I highly recommend that you do an "Integrity Checklist". Make a list of every area of your life in which you feel incomplete or have not finished a project; you have made promises but have not kept them; if there's an apology needed, or a misunderstanding that needs to be cleared… anything incomplete, you must complete.

This will not only "close the loop", but also it will also allow you to reset your "compass" and allow you to start anew.

Integrity is an "inside job". Allow yourself to feel completely integrous within and see the results without... its magic!

I personally thank YOU because the more that each of us chooses to live a life of integrity, the more that we will have a positive impact on this crazy world of ours... May you live the life of your dreams, which is a natural result of an intergroup life. Aloha Nui Loa...

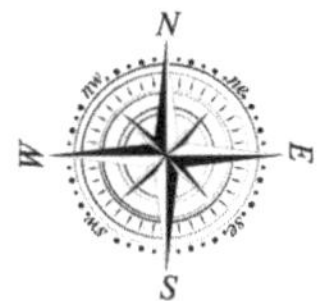

James Dentley on Integrity

The Unbreakable Chain of Integrity

At the core of human character, integrity is the unbreakable thread that weaves together honesty, ethics, and authenticity. It is the compass that guides us through life's labyrinth, lighting our path with unwavering principles. Just as if a ship relies on its anchor in choppy waters, our integrity grounds us in the face of challenges and temptation.

Integrity is not the declaration of perfection, but the commitment to staying true to one's values, even when the world tempts us to stray. It is standing tall when no one is watching and choosing the harder right over the easier wrong. This virtue is forged in the crucible of self-awareness – recognizing our strengths and acknowledging our weaknesses.

Imagine a world where every promise made is a promise kept, where words and actions are harmoniously aligned. Integrity shines like a beacon of light, casting out shadows of doubt and distrust. When integrity guides our decisions, it becomes a testament to our character, earning us the respect and admiration of those around us.

Integrity is a choice we make daily, a reflection of our inner compass. It is the courage to admit when we are wrong and the humility to learn from our mistakes. Every step taken with integrity builds bridges of trust and cultivates an atmosphere of accountability and credibility.

History's pages are filled with stories of individuals whose unwavering integrity transformed societies. Gandhi's commitment to nonviolence, Mandela's dedication to equality, and countless others who stood firm despite the odds, remind us that integrity is a beacon of hope in times of despair.

Yet, integrity is not reserved for the great leaders alone. It resides within each of us, waiting to be nurtured. It is the cashier who returns excess change, the student who resists cheating, the parent who leads by example. It is the collective choices of individuals that shape the character of a community.

In a world, that often values expediency over ethics, the flame of integrity burns brighter than ever. As we navigate the complexities of modern life, let us remember that integrity is not just a word, but also a way of life. It is the legacy we leave for future generations, a testament to our commitment to something greater than we are.

So, let integrity be our guiding star, a constant reminder of who we are and who we aspire to be. Let it be the force that propels us forward, unbroken and unyielding, through the tapestry of our lives. Never forget that your success and your example built with integrity can be someone else's miracle!

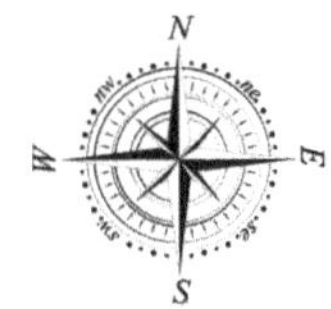

Joy Willett on Integrity

Wow, this is a complex word or theme, isn't it? What exactly IS Integrity, anyway?

By definition, it means:

1. A firm adherence to a code of especially moral or artistic values.

2. Incorruptibility.

3. An unimpaired condition: soundness.

Other definitions include being whole or complete.

So let's unpack this.

When we are "aligned" internally and even externally, with what is truly our personal set of values…nothing can shake us, can it? We can even feel a sense of passion and energy. Integrity in ourselves will have us acting the same way when we are being watched as when we are alone. In fact, this is another example of integrity.

When I am in integrity, I feel aligned. Whole. Balanced. Full of passion and energy. I am COMMITTED to my goals or actions 200%. I can be quietly exhibiting Integrity. In addition, I can also exhibit Integrity with a wonderful dynamic quality!

Integrity also feels like I am one with my Mission, my Purpose, my Vision, and my Heart. It has similar characteristics to "Courage" or "take heart". Yet is quiet like a Dove of Peace. It is as Strong as Spider's silk. It reaches to the bottom of the ocean floors and goes to the farthest Galaxies.

When I think of others who had Integrity, I think of Martin Luther King, Jr. and his unwavering integrity in walking the Path of Non-Violence for Civil or Human Rights for all.

I think of Gandhi with his peace-infused integrity, upholding his own moral compass to effect Change in India for those suffering inequality as a people.

I think of my own Father, who always did the "right thing" for others. In fact, at his memorial, I was amazed by his business colleagues who talked about my Dad, who I revered, and Dad's steadfastness to his principles…in his career as a high-level executive and as a father. I thought it almost strange that they would go out of their way to discuss this for others at the service to know about!

I think also about my own life and path. How I have usually "erred" on the side of Integrity according to my own inner compass of what is right…to the detriment of me receiving perhaps money and "recognition". However, I remained in Integrity with myself.

There is an old sports saying that goes like this: "It isn't whether you win or lose, its how you play the Game."

In our lives, think what a World we would exist in if we all moved through Life with a sense of "common" Integrity. Perhaps that is what religions have tried to create in our human societies: a moral code that can be adhered to and accepted. Even some democratic Governments too.

However, it might just be up to each one of us, to listen to our own "inner guidance systems" that keep us aligned with our Hearts and steering our Minds and thus Bodies!

I am game, how about You?

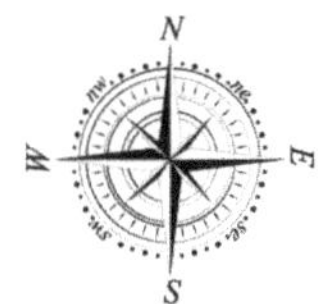

Julie Ann Meyer on Integrity

As a heart-centered entrepreneur, I have always believed that personal integrity is the cornerstone of success in both business and life. A quality not only shapes who we are as individuals but also has a profound impact on the people around us.

So, what exactly is personal integrity? Well, it is that unwavering commitment to our values, principles, and moral standards, regardless of external pressures or temptations. It is the foundation upon which we build trust with ourselves and then others. When we embody integrity, we align our actions with our beliefs and begin to trust ourselves.

Personal integrity is not just a solitary pursuit. It has a ripple effect that touches the lives of those around us. In the business world, this effect can be particularly powerful. When clients, customers, and team members see you consistently acting in alignment with your values, it breeds trust and respect. They know they can rely on you, and this trust is the bedrock of strong, enduring relationships.

Integrity also serves as a source of inspiration. When you lead with integrity, others are more likely to follow your example. As a heart-centered entrepreneur, you can inspire your team to share your values and mission, making them passionate about their work. It is like a domino effect of positivity and purpose.

However, the magic of personal integrity does not stop there. It is magnetic. When you hold fast to your values, you naturally attract like-minded individuals into your orbit. These are the people who resonate with your mission and values, and who want to be part of your journey. It is not just about networking; it is about forming deep, meaningful connections.

This magnetism is rooted in authenticity. People are naturally drawn to those who are genuine, transparent, and true to themselves. In a world that often seems driven by superficiality, authenticity is a refreshing and magnetic quality. When you maintain your integrity, you exhibit authenticity. You are not pretending to be someone you are not, and this genuineness attracts others who appreciate your realness.

In a world where many hide behind veils and pretenses, your genuine self-burns brightly, attracting those in search of a real connection. These people will resonate with you, follow your journey, and become devoted clients, partners, or collaborators.

However, the power of personal integrity goes beyond professional relationships. It extends into every facet of our lives. When you live with integrity, you experience a profound sense of inner peace. There is no internal struggle because your thoughts, actions, and beliefs are in harmony. You can look at yourself in the mirror and know that you are staying true to your values, and that is a priceless feeling.

Moreover, personal integrity is your guiding compass in times of uncertainty. When faced with tough decisions, you can turn to your values and principles for guidance. They provide clarity in the midst of chaos, ensuring that your choices are consistent with your beliefs.

In a world that sometimes seems to encourage shortcuts and bending the rules, integrity can be your anchor. It reminds you to take the high road, even when it is the more challenging path. In addition, it is precisely that commitment to doing what is right, rather than what is easy, that sets you apart in both personal and professional arenas.

So, how do we cultivate personal integrity and make it a central part of our lives? It starts with self-reflection. Take the time to identify your core values and principles. What matters most to you? What are the guiding lights of your life? Once you have pinpointed these, hold them close to your heart and let them guide your actions.

Next, practice mindfulness. Be aware of your choices and actions throughout the day. Are they in alignment with your values? Are you staying true to yourself, even in the face of challenges? Being conscious of your decisions is the first step towards living with integrity.

Additionally, surround yourself with individuals who share your values and encourage your commitment to personal integrity. These friends and colleagues will not only support your journey but also hold you accountable when you falter.

Remember that personal integrity is not about being perfect. We all make mistakes and face moments of weakness. What matters is your commitment to self-correction and growth. When you slip, acknowledge it, learn from it, and use it as an opportunity to reinforce your integrity.

In the grand scheme of things, personal integrity is not just a character trait; it is a way of life. It is about being true to yourself and your values, even when the world seems to push you in a different direction. It is about inspiring trust, building meaningful relationships, and staying on the path of authenticity.

As a heart-centered entrepreneur, I cannot emphasize enough how integral personal integrity is to our journey. The compass keeps us on course. It is the difference between fleeting success and a legacy of impact. So, let us embrace personal integrity and let it guide us to a brighter, more authentic future.

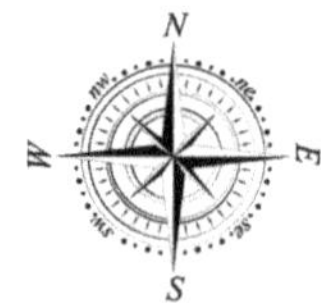

Kenyelle Ash on Integrity

Let us embark on a journey into the heart of integrity and delve into the profound concept that "Your Reputation Precedes You" - a motto that has guided me throughout my career and life. The essence of a remarkable reputation lies in one's integrity, as it shapes the foundation of our name and defines the legacy we leave behind.

I vividly recall my time as a partner at a brand management and engagement firm back in 2012. It was then that I truly grasped the significance of conducting ourselves with unwavering integrity. In our line of work, where professional talent management is paramount, we understood that our reputation was everything. "All you have is your name," as the age-old adage goes.

The pursuit of integrity is multifaceted. It involves not only the quality of the work we produce but also the way we communicate with clients, colleagues, and partners. Every interaction, every email, and every promise must exude professionalism. It is imperative that we refrain from overpromising and under-delivering; instead, we should aspire to under promise and over deliver, a practice that resonates with honesty and reliability.

As we climb the ladder of success, it becomes evident that falsehoods and dishonesty are not prerequisites for advancement. One need not resort to lies, cheating, or disparaging others in order to progress. The true goal is to have one's work, work ethic, and the quality of one's output speak for itself.

Throughout our professional journeys, we have likely encountered individuals who made grandiose promises they could not fulfill. We have also crossed paths with those who feigned experience and accomplishments to secure business opportunities. Such an approach, however, is destined to unravel, as it exposes a lack of authenticity and a dearth of quality in one's work.

In a world where our name is our most cherished asset, we must also be discerning about the associations we form. This involves not only evaluating the quality of people's work but also the nature of their relationships. There is nothing more disheartening than vouching for someone, entrusting him or her with a task, only to witness their inability to meet the professional standards expected. Your customers and clients rely on you to deliver a promised level of quality, a promise that forms the basis of your brand.

In light of this, it becomes apparent that operating with integrity is the key to fulfilling these promises. It entails being who you claim to be and doing precisely what you say you will do.

Here are Five Fundamental Ways to Ensure That Your Reputation Truly Precedes You:

1. **Do What You Say You Will:** The cornerstone of integrity is keeping your word. Being a person of your word means committing to your promises and following through with unwavering dedication. It is the embodiment of reliability and trustworthiness.

2. **Be Authentic:** Honesty is the path to authenticity. Never exaggerate your skills or connections to gain an advantage in business. Being genuine about your abilities and your network not only builds trust but also prevents the eventual collapse of any exaggerated claims.

3. **Under promise and over-deliver:** As a testament to your integrity, set realistic expectations. Overpromising and under delivering is a surefire way to erode trust. Instead, under promise, and then exceed expectations, leaving a lasting positive impression.

4. **Uplift, Don't Undermine:** A person of integrity does not resort to speaking ill of others or their work to gain an edge in business. Focus on your strengths, abilities, and the problems you can solve. Build your reputation by uplifting others and highlighting your unique value.

5. **Be Selective in Associations:** Your name is closely tied to the individuals and entities you associate with. Be mindful of whom you attach

your name to and whom you allow to associate with yours. Use discernment; evaluate the quality of their work and the integrity of their relationships before forging connections.

In summary, integrity is the bedrock upon which your reputation is built. Upholding the principles of honesty, authenticity, and reliability will ensure that your name is synonymous with excellence, trustworthiness, and success, ultimately allowing your reputation to precede you in all your endeavors.

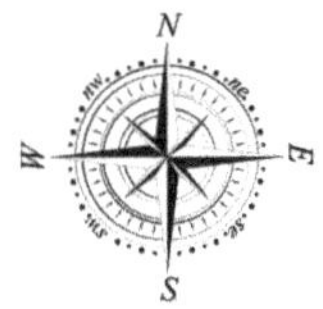

Leslie Kuntz on Integrity

The Soul Essence of Integrity

Admiring the orange glow of the harvest moon, the wheat fields were turning a golden hue as the sun set while we were making the rounds checking the crops. Standing in front of our truck was the neighbor, talking to my dad with the glow of the wheat field behind them. I could only see them shaking hands and nodding heads. When my dad got back in the pickup, I asked, "Dad, why did you shake hands with him and both nod your heads, you see him all the time?"

My dad replied, "His harvester broke down, and his crops are ahead of mine. He wants to use my combine, and when he takes the grain to the elevator, he will get funds for the parts he needs. I told him yes, and that he could repay me by helping me sometime."

"What are funds?" I questioned. "It is another word for money," replied my dad. "How do you know he will give your combine back or really come and help you?" I asked.

"You asked about the handshake and the nod of our heads. Well, that is a gentlemen's agreement. It is a promise that we will do the best that we can to help each other. It's our promise based on our integrity." My dad replied. "Is integrity another word for money too?"

My dad laughed, "No, Integrity is much more valuable than money. It is a person's soul essence, something money cannot buy. It's our promise from our heart, mind and soul that we will do the best we can for ourselves and others, always."

Later that week, we were on the way to the grain elevator with our crop. Everyone was in a hurry to get the crop delivered before the rain. We were next in line, and I noticed my dad waving in a smaller rickety old truck in front of us.

"Dad!" I exclaimed! "I thought you said we were in a hurry to drop the load and get back for another, why would you let him in front of us?"

"You notice the size of his truck and the size of ours?" My dad replied. "He has to make twice as many trips as we do to get his crops sold and in the elevator. Someone did the same for me in the past." "Is that using Integrity?" I asked.

He laughed, "Yes, helping others is a form of integrity. It's taking the time to make a good decision when the opportunity arises for the greater good of others." Driving home, even when nobody was around, he kept using the blinker in the grain truck. Laughing aloud "You're being silly dad! Nobody can see you using the blinkers!"

"Being in the habit of always doing the right things, even when nobody is watching, is very important. Integrity is not something you turn off and on; it's your internal compass of right and wrong." He replied.

"You have to be your own compass in your heart to keep your mind, body, and soul from getting lost."

These were just a few of the lessons I learned about integrity growing up from my dad. He is my shining example of integrity.

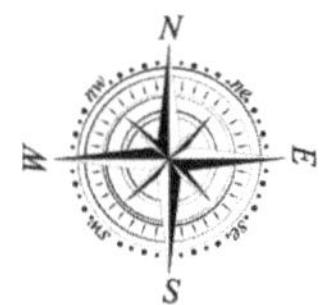

Loretta Wetzel on integrity

Business Brilliance: The Transformative Power of Integrity

"It's never simply about how much privilege and power you have; it's always about how you use it integrally for the advancement of humanity."

Legacy builders, entrepreneurs, and dreamers—welcome to the heart of the matter. A journey where we delve not into the superficialities of profit margins or strategies, but into the lifeblood of a truly transformative business: integrity. While some see it as a moral compass (and there is no denying its roots in that realm), business brilliance is illuminated through integrity as an essential and pragmatic cornerstone for achieving long-term success.

Why Integrity Makes Good Business Sense

Integrity is not synonymous with flawlessness. We are bound by our human intricacies, often entangled in our own imperfections. Yet, when promises break or commitments wane, success lies in the swift, soulful acknowledgment of our missteps, feeling their resonance, and recalibrating. Through candid conversations, even colossal debacles like Enron or the FTX cryptocurrency calamity could have been sidestepped. The rich tapestry of integrity unfolds through several threads, of which three shimmer most vividly and each tied to components of running a successful business.

A Legacy Built on Integrity Through Identity

Wake up everybody and understand this: your business is an extension of your identity. Every choice you make today echoes in the annals of your legacy. But what if you have challenges with your identity? Individuals usually fall into one of three categories if their belief system is at a lower vibrational frequency.

Category #1 – Born in adversity, some believe destiny has shackled them. In other words, it is impossible to rise above the socio-economic status they were born into because generationally, that is just the way it is. To them, remember Henry Ford's words: "Whether you think you can or you can't, you're right."

Category #2 - Others grapple with internal scars, fearing unmasking their genuine selves would tarnish love and success. Nevertheless, embracing and healing these scars can rebirth a business. There is NOTHING in life that is not redeemable if you truly believe in forgiveness.

Category #3 - Lastly, the haunting whisper, "I am not good enough…" Yet, we are woven from a fabric of abundance, deserving of prosperity. My journey, from the tremors of corporate layoffs to triumphant entrepreneurship, serves as a testament.

When I lost my corporate America six-figure income job impacted by layoffs. I had three strikes against me – graced with age, competing against millennials accepting job offers one-third of my salary, and having two children in college with out-of-state tuition. **Ouch!**

Little did I realize this was the pathway to considering entrepreneurship and I took the leap. Fast forward thirteen years later; I am a successful serial entrepreneur with multiple businesses in the fields of real estate investing and family entrepreneur coaching.

So how do you shatter these glass ceilings of self-limitation?

1. **Drop your ego and significance.** They are achievement killers based on usage and not inherently bad. When you shed ego's weight, clarity and introspection appear.
2. **Be willing to stand in the space of "nothing."** Cultivate moments of stillness, for within them springs forth the wellspring of innovation.

Consistency is the key. If some issue keeps popping up and you are unable to quiet your mind that is a clue to look for where you are out of integrity in your personal or business life. Get in communication and clean it up.

3. **Create new possibilities**. Dream with fervor. With clarity, etch vibrant dreams on the canvas of the mind, and then chase them with passion. You cannot create something new at a low vibrational frequency full of noise, distractions, and broken promises. Now that your space is clear, your new possibilities should fill you with excitement and joy! Then, take the necessary zone action to go get it!

What I have just described is really your freedom ticket to successful everyday living. When you consistently engage in the above behaviors, you are living an integral life.

Relationships are built through shared experiences where there is a mutual exchange of value. When a business consistently demonstrates integrity, it sends a clear message: "You can trust us." This is the brand magnetism of integrity. Trust is not just an emotion; it is a tangible asset that influences purchasing decisions, fosters loyalty, and can be the decisive factor that tips the scale in your favor during competitive bidding and influence mastery.

When I co-created the **We Do the Impossible** movement with my business partner and husband of 40+ years, the mission statement became clear: to empower the next generation of dreamers to do the impossible.

The focus is on STEMM education so that students will be able to have a competitive edge in the private space tourism industry for employment. As leaders of this movement, we are bidding to become the first African American married couple to go into sub-orbital space, imagine the outpouring of support from relationships built over the years. Businesses are supporting us because they believe in what we stand for and trust we will get the job done. More importantly, it is a vision of hope for America. It is a vision where people still matter, their dreams, and desires still matter, and the only way we will get there is through the transformative power of integrity.

Integrity is not just a moral compass; it is a compass that directs your business to sustainable success. It is the golden thread that weaves through every facet of your business, strengthening your brand, elevating your workforce, fostering customer loyalty, mitigating risks, clarifying decisions, and attracting quality partnerships.

It is time for us, the architects of legacies, the dreamers and builders of the future, to embrace integrity as our guiding star. To create businesses that are not just profitable but also admirable. So, let us ask ourselves: Are we ready to unlock the transformative power of integrity in our journey to business brilliance? The answer is unequivocally YES!

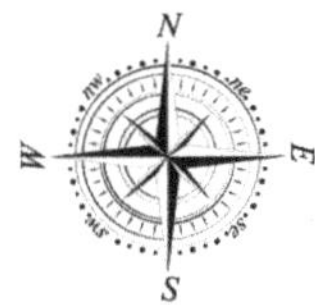

Lori McNeil on integrity

Nurturing a Lasting Legacy: The Essence of Integrity Leadership in Business

In the dynamic and ever-evolving landscape of the business world, one constant remains irreplaceable: integrity leadership. As a seasoned business strategist consultant and coach, I have had the privilege of witnessing firsthand the transformative power of leaders who exemplify unwavering honesty, ethics, and moral principles. Let us delve into the facets of integrity leadership, exploring its significance in fostering a legacy that extends far beyond the bottom line.

At the core of integrity, leadership lies a commitment to honesty and transparency. In an age where information travels at the speed of light, businesses are under constant scrutiny. Integrity leaders must embrace openness in communication, making it the cornerstone of their interactions. Being forthright and candid, these leaders cultivate environments of trust that trickle down through the organizational hierarchy. This culture of transparency enhances internal collaboration as well as the brand's reputation in the eyes of customers, partners, and stakeholders.

Ethical decision-making stands as another pillar of integrity leadership. Business landscapes are riddled with complex choices, and integrity leaders navigate these intricacies by anchoring their decisions in ethical considerations. In my consulting practice, it is important to evaluate the long-term consequences of decisions rather than succumbing to short-lived gains. This approach should align with the company's values and contribute to sustainable success, stimulating a legacy of responsible leadership.

Consistency, an attribute cherished by integrity leaders, ensures that principles and values are not mere buzzwords but guiding stars. The leaders I have worked with understand that their actions, behaviors, and decisions must mirror their moral compass. This steadfast commitment to consistency cultivates a sense of predictability and reliability, both internally and externally. Team members feel secure in knowing their leaders will uphold the same ethical standards, promoting a culture of dedication and loyalty that transcends organizational boundaries.

Integrity leaders possess a rare quality of accountability – an acknowledgment of both successes and failures. I have witnessed how these leaders take ownership of their actions, even when mistakes occur. This practice not only enhances their credibility but also showcases a willingness to learn and improve. When embracing accountability, integrity leaders inspire their teams to take responsibility, creating an environment where innovation flourishes, and lessons are embraced rather than avoided.

A cornerstone of integrity leadership is a profound respect for others. Through empathy, fairness, and inclusivity, these leaders create a workplace where diversity is celebrated, and collaboration thrives. This approach enhances team cohesion and resonates with customers and partners, strengthening relationships that contribute to the organization's legacy.

Courage is the fuel that propels integrity leaders to take a stand for what is right, even when faced with adversity. I often remind my clients that the business world can be fraught with ethical dilemmas, and it takes a resolute leader to navigate these treacherous waters. By fearlessly confronting wrongdoing and injustice, integrity leaders showcase their commitment to a higher purpose, inspiring others to follow suit. This courage, rooted in unwavering principles, is a beacon that guides the organization's path toward a legacy of meaningful impact.

Trustworthiness, earned through consistent ethical behavior, is the lifeblood of integrity leadership. It is the foundation upon which relationships are built, both within and outside the organization. Remember, trust is not easily earned, but its value is immeasurable, integrity leaders prioritize trust-building at every turn, cultivating an atmosphere of reliability that resonates with stakeholders, customers, and partners alike.

While the pursuit of short-term gains may offer fleeting success, integrity leaders possess the wisdom to focus on the long-term perspective. When leaders shun shortcuts in favor of a sustainable trajectory and instead prioritize values over immediate profits, they lay the groundwork for a legacy that is characterized by responsible growth and positive impact.

The connection between integrity, leadership, and the creation of legacy is undeniable. Businesses guided by integrity leaders leave an indelible mark on their industries, setting standards that transcend financial metrics. Integrity leadership is not a choice, but a responsibility. By embodying these principles, leaders lay the foundation for a legacy that extends far beyond their tenure. In a world craving authentic and principled leadership, integrity stands as the compass that guides businesses toward a brighter and more impactful future.

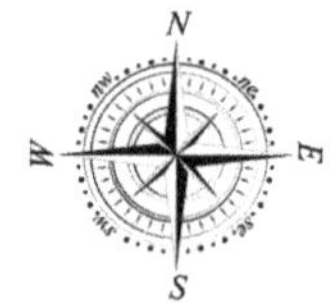

M Teresa Lawrence on integrity

"Dreams are seedlings of all achievements."
–Napoleon Hill

Have you ever seen a child joyously at play? The playground is an infinite universe of possibilities. The sandbox is a glorious beach. The jungle gym is an epic mountain ready to be conquered. And the slide? Oh my, what an opportunity to slide down a waterfall into new adventures. The joy of grand adventures is palpable on the playground. Imagination, belief, intention, action, and inevitability are all at play in creating magic. Do you remember what it feels like to play and create magic?

Pretend for a moment that you are a child, and you are discovering the power of words to create different realities. Say this aloud: "Today, I choose to be glorious!" This simple sentence is so powerful. Look at it. Read it. Dissect it. It starts with the word, "today," emphatically points out that I have made a choice and denotes the focus of my thoughts as a state of being that is glorious. Words are so magical, aren't they?

Take for example the word "today." It magically references time, and the time is now, ongoing during the course of the day, today! Remember, life happens in the NOW!

If you are wondering how long I can discuss the intricacies of one simple sentence, be prepared to experience a joyous ride into the realm of creative leadership. Words are magical and when used intentionally have the power to manifest. Today, I choose to be glorious! Please say those words aloud.

The next word at play in the sentence is the word "choose." I could have chosen to be anything. That is the point. The moment we declare with clarity our intention, we give our minds permission to focus on that intention. During the course of your day, consciously choose your thoughts and direct them towards your purpose. Today, I choose to be glorious! Again, say those words aloud.

Do you have a definite purpose in life? A goal that fills your mind with joy and passion. On the other hand, are you presently experiencing life in what is commonly referred to as the drift? The drift keeps you focused on the past or somehow projecting experiences from the past into the future. I have spent a lot of time in the drift daydreaming of my future greatness and worrying about things that happened in the past. What did I create during this time? NOTHING! Life is now. It is happening today. Today, I choose to be glorious! By now, I hope you are saying this aloud automatically.

In The Science of Personal Achievement, Napoleon Hill points out "Human thoughts have a tendency to transform themselves into their physical equivalent." He also points out that the "only thing over which any human being complete unquestionable control has is the power of thought." Isn't that amazing? Today, I choose to be glorious!

Do you know what you want? I am quite sure that you already know what you do not want. The reason I know is that I often ask people what they want, and they list off all the things they do not want. Will you be able to get what you want if you are focusing on what you do not want? Dreams are the seedlings of all achievement; they spring forth from your imagination and call upon you to choose and declare your purpose. Today, I choose to be glorious!

What does the sentence mean to you? What do you really want? Answer as if you were a child filled with dreams and a firm belief that you can do anything. I believe that is where we find our strength and lead with integrity into an amazing future.

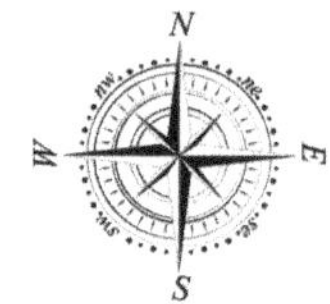

Marie Diamond on Integrity

Harnessing the Power of Feng Shui for Integrity
–Driven Leadership

As a Feng Shui Master, I have always appreciated the significance of our surroundings. My days are packed – from consulting A-list clients to leading online workshops. No matter how hectic things get, I consistently prioritize a clean and positive workspace. Why? Because a harmonious environment directly impacts our success.

Feng Shui is an Ancient Chinese energy system all about maintaining a positive flow of energy, or "chi", in your home and workspace. By putting the right items in the right places and by activating your Personal Directions, you can use this flow of energy in order to make your dreams a reality.

Here, I will share insights on how Feng Shui principles have not only transformed spaces but also enhanced leadership qualities:

Eliminate the Chaos: One of the first things I emphasize is decluttering. It is not just about a tidy space. It is about clearing your mind, making space for new ideas, and enhancing the flow of positive energy. When our environment is clear, so is our vision as leaders.

Position for Perception: I have always stressed the "power position" in Feng Shui. It is crucial for leaders to be positioned in a way that they can perceive opportunities, and threats, and maintain an open dialogue with their teams.

Seek Support and Grounding: A sturdy chair is not just furniture; it is a symbol of support and grounding. Leaders need a solid foundation, whether it is in the form of supportive teams, a clear vision, or, in Feng Shui terms, a high-backed chair that gives a feeling of authority and protection.

Find Your Direction: Every individual has a unique energy that guides them towards success, good health, relationships, and wisdom. Just as I guide people to find their Success Direction in Feng Shui, leaders should find and focus on their vision, and their unique path to success.

Activate Your Leadership Potential: The objects and symbols we surround ourselves with have power. For me, it is about using symbols of power in Feng Shui to manifest dreams.

Symbols of power are crucial in amplifying our intentions and manifesting our aspirations. For leaders, it means aligning their workspace with symbols, achievements, and reminders of their goals and aspirations.

These can include images of successful individuals in your field or those who have realized similar goals to yours. Pictures of your idols and heroes also serve as strong motivators. Additionally, proudly displaying any certificates or awards you have earned can be a testament to your accomplishments.

For some, religious or spiritual figures provide grounding and guidance. Even playful symbols, like a mock Oscar trophy with your name, or a photoshopped magazine cover featuring you, can inspire ambition and visualization. Moreover, displaying your company's logos or marketing materials can serve as a daily reminder of your professional purpose and journey.

For leaders looking to steer their teams with authenticity and integrity, Feng Shui offers more than just spatial arrangement; it provides insights into balance, harmony, and alignment of purpose. I believe that as leaders align their external surroundings with their internal goals, they can lead with greater clarity, purpose, and, most importantly, integrity.

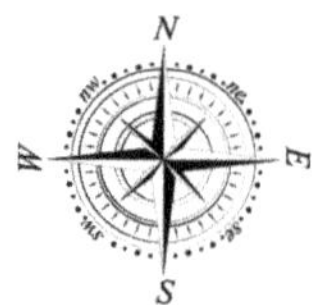

Michael Silvers on Integrity

In the myriad roles I've undertaken — from the disciplined paths of an LAPD officer and a medical professional to the dynamic world of personal development, working alongside legends like T. Harv Eker — the bedrock of all my endeavors has always been integrity. As the leader of The Mentor Studio, I have had the privilege of guiding and connecting with some of the world's foremost thought leaders. This journey has reinforced a truth I have held dear all my life: integrity is not just a virtue; it is the very foundation upon which impactful lives are built.

My years in law enforcement taught me about the weight of responsibility and the importance of ethical decision-making. On the streets of Los Angeles, every decision, every action, had consequences that extended far beyond myself. It was a realm where integrity was not just a moral choice; it was a lifeline, for myself and for those I was sworn to protect.

Transitioning into the medical field, I was thrust into a world where trust and honesty were not just valued, but vital. Patients entrusted their lives to our care, a responsibility that demanded the utmost sincerity and integrity. This experience ingrained in me an unwavering commitment to truth and ethics, principles I carried forward into the realm of personal development.

In working with T. Harv Eker and other luminaries in the personal development industry, I have witnessed firsthand how integrity forms the backbone of true leadership and lasting impact. These experiences have only deepened my conviction that a leader's first duty is to the truth — to themselves, their team, and their mission.

At The Mentor Studio, where we connect people with mentors who can transform their lives and businesses, the principle of integrity is paramount. It is not just about teaching skills or sharing knowledge; it is about fostering relationships built on trust, respect, and honesty. Our mentors are not just teachers; they are beacons of integrity, guiding our clients not just towards success, but also towards a life of meaning and ethical substance.

I have learned that integrity in leadership is about consistency — aligning actions with words and making decisions that reflect one's deepest values and principles. It is about being the same person in the boardroom as you are at home. It is about admitting mistakes and being accountable. This consistency is what builds trust, and trust is what builds teams, businesses, and movements that can change the world.

In conclusion, my journey through diverse fields has taught me that while skills and knowledge are crucial, it is integrity that truly makes a leader. It is the thread that weaves together the tapestry of a life well lived and a career marked by impact and purpose. As leaders, mentors, and human beings striving to make a difference, let us hold fast to integrity, for it is the compass that guides us to our true north in both life and business.

Michelle McClain on Integrity

What if I told you integrity is the bridge between where you are and where you want to be?

Better health? Yes. Better romance? Yes. Better income? Yes. How about improved partnerships, a healthier environment, or a happier family? Yes- all the above. Your results in life are directly related to the role integrity plays in it. The keys to a life of richness and fulfillment are in the hands of a person who lives with integrity.

When one lives in integrity and alignment with their word, life can have a consistent, at-ease flow. Picture integrity being like a wheel of life. In that wheel, there are spokes that help it go 'round. Each spoke keeps the wheel of life in perfect, healthy balance to function, 'go-round', and get to its desired life destinations. When one of the spokes is broken, aka an area of life is out of integrity, the wheel/tire cannot spin around correctly. It now has a glitch, and the wheel of life struggles to go around. This broken spoke affects the rotation of how the entire wheel (of life) turns. When we are out of integrity in our lives, it is like having a broken spoke, and our lives do not function at the healthy rate that they could. Instead, it is slower, more challenging, inconsistent, untrustworthy, frustrating, essentially broken, and leads us down an undesirable path. At the same time, the tire that is in complete integrity spins solid and adequately, with ease ebb and flow.

Integrity means to keep our word and commitments, both to ourselves and to others. Some simple examples of being in integrity to oneself look like waking up when we said we would, sticking to the diet plan, and showing up to the gym when we said we would, making the phone call, or having that conversation we said we would. Its living in alignment with and following through with our word.

Integrity affects us individually and, as a whole on a higher consciousness level. Not only does this allow us to receive what we desire in our personal lives, but also it supports the evolution of the planet when we live in integrity. By showing up where you say you are going to show up, you allow the manifestation to unfold.

For example, one thing I teach my sales team is when you have planned to show up to XYZ location at XYZ time, now your Higher Power can align your new client there to meet you. That is when these beautiful synchronicities in life happen. We think these magical moments are coincidental or accidental, but in fact, these can be designed. When we create a plan, act in alignment with our word (integrity), the miracle happens! Now not only are you moving towards your personal goal, but also you met the person who desired your services to further their current life goals- thus the evolution of the planet (all of our goals being met) and flow of life continues. We are helping one another succeed in this case, by being our word, being in integrity, and following through with what we say we are going to do.

The goals and dreams that are within you, some would argue, were strategically placed there by The Creator, because you have the capabilities to bring these visions into the world. That said by following through, and being in integrity with the goals and dreams you decide to pursue, you are adding to the planet's evolution. And, on the opposite end of the spectrum, by not being in integrity and failing to keep your word to what you say you're going to do, you stop to this process of evolution through you.

"In the beginning was the word."- As an old scripture says, it is the opening to a manifestation. Walking in integrity with the word that you declare, is how the manifestation materializes. Many fail to have their dreams manifest because they are walking out of alignment with their word and what they say they're going to do about the desired outcome. Integrity is the 'following through' portion of the goal actualizing. It could also be seen as the self-management and self-discipline portion of goal attainment.

Integrity affects a wide range of characteristics within us. Characteristics such as courage, self-worth, our ability to trust ourselves and have confidence in who we are. Having integrity with oneself is a major key to building self-confidence and self-trust- Because you know that you can count on yourself.

You know that you can trust you, to follow through, to show up, to lead the way, to get it done. Integrity with oneself is the best ways to build unshakeable character and courage. All else builds from there.

In closing- The world one desires, on a direct, interpersonal level and a higher consciousness level, exists in the hands of integrity. Decide what you want in all areas of life, plan to attain it, and walk that path in integrity. You will receive the desires of your heart and support the evolution of the planet overall.

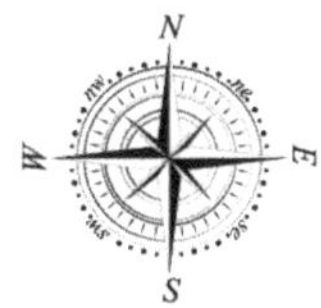

Dr. Michelle Odette Green on Integrity

Why is integrity so important? Well, imagine you are building a house. Integrity is the foundation of the house. Without it, the whole structure crumbles. It is the anchor of trust, the cornerstone of respect, and the secret sauce to success.

As an entrepreneur, author, coach, mother, wife, and grandmother, my journey through life has taught me invaluable lessons about the true meaning and importance of integrity. Integrity begins with an authentic understanding of who you are and what you stand for.

To put integrity further into perspective, ask yourself this question. If an invisible person followed you around all day, what would they see? Would they see you keeping your word? Would they see you honoring your agreements? Would they see you being fair in your dealings? Would they see you being truthful in your interactions with others?

Integrity is not just a fancy word to toss around. It is a guiding principle that permeates every facet of your being. It extends beyond ethical behavior; it encompasses your relationships, your personal growth, your professional growth, and your contributions to the world at large. Living with integrity is a journey, not a destination. ***It is a way of life!***

It is about being true to yourself, living by your principles, and standing up for what you believe in. It is like the backbone of your character, the compass that guides your actions, and the mirror that reflects your authenticity.

Nevertheless, let's get real, shall we? It is not always easy to be a person of integrity. Sometimes, the truth can be uncomfortable, even scary. But remember, every time you choose truth over convenience; you are not only helping yourself but also empowering others to do the same.

Integrity begins with living in alignment with your core values. Whether you are an employee, entrepreneur, parent, coach, spouse, in a relationship or in any other role, your values define who you are and guide your actions. By identifying and embracing your values, you can ensure that your choices and decisions align with your true self.

Reflect on your core values and assess how well your daily life reflects them. Are your thoughts, words, and actions in harmony with what you hold dear? This self-awareness is the first step towards living a life of integrity.

Ever heard the saying, "Honesty is the best policy?" Well, it is more than just a wise saying. It is a recipe for stronger relationships, better communication, and personal and professional growth. And guess what is more? It is also a ticket to freedom - freedom from fear, deceit, and dishonesty. It liberates you from the fear and chains of lies, deceit, and dishonesty.

Imagine this: you are carrying a heavy backpack filled with stones. Each stone represents a lie or a deceit. How would you feel? Now, imagine removing each stone, one by one. That is the freedom honesty can give you.

Take responsibility for your choices, both the good and the not so good. Have the courage to admit your mistakes and the grace to forgive yourself and others. Use your mistakes as opportunities for growth and self-improvement.

Below are some actionable strategies that can help you strengthen your integrity:

1. **Embrace Your Authentic Self:** It is easy to wear masks, to play roles that others expect of you. That is like being a chameleon, constantly changing colors to blend in. Embrace who you are, quirks and all. It

is your uniqueness that makes you, YOU! As you evolve, you become more comfortable in your own skin and feel less need to put on a mask.

2. **Cultivate Self-Awareness:** You can't fix what you don't know is broken, right? Take some time for self-reflection or reflective thinking. Understand your motives, your actions, and your values. It is like taking a magnifying glass to your soul.

3. **Speak Your Truth, Even When Your Voice Shakes:** It is easy to nod along, to avoid rocking the boat. But remember, a smooth sea never made a skilled sailor. Stand up for what you believe in, even if you are standing alone.

4. **Practice Radical Honesty:** Honesty is not just about not lying. It is about being brutally honest with yourself. It is about acknowledging your flaws, your mistakes, and your failures. It is about owning your story, the good, the bad, and the ugly.

5. **Walk the Talk:** It is easy to preach, but actions speak louder than words. Let your actions reflect your words. Be the change you wish to see in the world.

Now, I am not saying it is going to be easy. There will be days when you will be tempted to take the easy way out. However, remember, integrity is choosing your thoughts, words, and actions based on your values rather than personal gain. It is about doing the right thing, even when no one is watching.

In the end, integrity is not just about what you do. It is about who you are. And, who you want to be. Living with integrity is easier in the long run. You will be more respected and experience more success.

Live with integrity. Live with authenticity. Live with purpose. Because you are worth it!

Misty Kerrigan on Integrity

Developing your Navigational Instrument for Life

The cultivation of a well-developed moral compass is widely recognized as pivotal for personal growth, the cultivation of trust in interpersonal relationships, and the positive contribution to society. This crucial facet facilitates adept navigation through moral quandaries, fostering decisions that harmonize with one's deeply held values. However, a question that lingered in my mind, particularly through the early stages of my professional journey, was the intricate process of determining one's direction akin to the cardinal points found in a conventional compass.

This contemplation led me to ponder whether individuals are inherently endowed with an innate "True North" or if the orientation of this internal compass is an evolving construct shaped by life experiences. If the latter holds true, the subsequent query arises: from where does one commence this profound and introspective journey?

During my early twenties, while engaged in employment at a residential treatment center catering to at-risk youth, this inquiry took on tangible significance. The center, an encompassing 24-hour therapeutic program, served as a haven for youth contending with a myriad of challenges. These challenges emanated from dysfunctional family environments, socioeconomic constraints, and traumatic experiences, which collectively left these young individuals feeling lost and disoriented in life. Such disorientation manifested in detrimental decision-making, diminished self-value, and a pervasive absence of self-trust.

Our approach, therefore, was to initiate the process of rebuilding their moral compass within an environment that fostered the establishment of self-integrity. Self-integrity, defined as the reconstruction of a sense of wholeness and unity within one's character by remaining steadfastly true to personal values and standards, became our guiding principle.

The inaugural step in this transformative journey involved the implementation of a structured formula. This entailed encouraging the youth to make incremental commitments and exhibit consistent behavior over time, culminating in the achievement of micro goals. The foundational premise underlying this process was the cultivation of an understanding that "their word" carried significant weight. Essentially, we embarked on the reconstruction of their lives by establishing an integral foundation, emphasizing the importance of honoring commitments not merely for external validation but principally for the cultivation of self-trust and personal identity.

The concept of self-integrity assumes a pivotal role in the comprehensive exploration of integrity and moral compasses. Defined by the unwavering consistency and alignment of one's actions with personal ethical principles, self-integrity embodies a steadfast commitment to upholding individual values across a spectrum of diverse contexts.

It is essential to recognize that a solid foundation of integrity is a common thread woven through these varied contexts. The need for such a foundation arises from the imperative of cultivating self-trust, a process that does not commence with external communication but, more significantly, with the internal dialogue we maintain with ourselves.

A pertinent example underscores the essence of this internal integrity. The act of keeping one's word transcends its role in establishing credibility with others; it serves as a paramount mechanism for building credibility within oneself. This intrinsic credibility becomes the cornerstone for fostering self-trust, thereby contributing to the elevation of self-value and confidence. In essence, the cultivation of self-integrity initiates a transformative journey that underscores the significance of internal consistency and ethical adherence in shaping an individual's character and sense of self-worth.

Subsequently, my professional trajectory diverged from the realm of residential treatment centers and at-risk youth. Instead, it steered me towards the spheres of moral compasses and self-integrity. These experiences became pivotal in shaping my career in leadership consulting, training, and academic writing, where the term "integrity" adorns walls, resonates in mission statements, and is strategically inserted into negotiations to influence outcomes. Regrettably, I must acknowledge that, on numerous occasions, the true essence of integrity is obscured, replaced by the hollowness of a mere token.

Consequently, I have arrived at the realization that the question of whether we are inherently imbued with an innate "True North" or if our internal compass undergoes evolution through life experiences becomes secondary. Similar to the routine maintenance required by a conventional compass, rectifying and recalibrating our moral compass is imperative. In the intricate tapestry of life, this rectification process can be as straightforward as aligning our speech with our genuine intentions and, most significantly, honoring the commitments we make to ourselves.

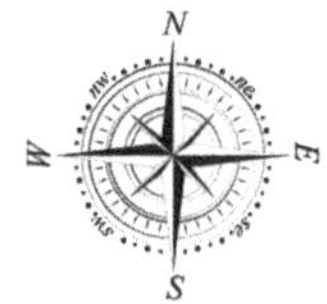

Moirar Leveille on Integrity

Leading with integrity as a holistic practitioner

*"To give real service you must add something which cannot be bought
or measured with money, and that is sincerity and integrity"*
– Douglas Adams

We are always serving, be it to others, ourselves, or a community through our work. We are always serving and how we do, it precedes us. Regardless of your professional background, your actions speak for you. Their words reverberate back to who you are and the quality of work you put out. It is through these actions that we touch people's hearts affecting their beliefs, attitudes, and productivity. Therefore, in a profession such as health care where more than people's lives are on the line, we cannot afford to gamble with integrity.

Integrity is simply being honest with yourself and others while upholding sound moral principles. It has to come from the self-first; a deep sense of self is the fertile ground from which integrity sprouts and those that eat of its fruits are both the bearer and anyone who nears its shade. There are two types; personal integrity and professional integrity. Personal integrity forms a base unto which professional integrity is built from and this inspires the employees to do their part diligently. A leader in any field needs to have both if the organization is to succeed.

Leaders with integrity in the medical field must practice the unyielding principle of standing for the truth despite the circumstances. This may look like a doctor making sure that a needy patient gets immediate life-saving treatment despite the fact that the hospital rules may demand otherwise. Sometimes one has to lay down what they believe is right in order to uphold the patient's beliefs/morals like not resuscitating when the patient has a DNR (Do Not Resuscitate) order. Tough choices are to be made but by respecting the people we serve and lead, we exude trustworthiness, reliability, and dependability.

My professional integrity started before I became a functional medical practitioner. Counter-intuitively, Graves' disease taught me to take care of myself by respecting my body enough to give it what it needs to recuperate despite what I felt. I developed values such as doing what I say when I say it and being a unique frame that defied all societal boxes for my own wellness. From that came a wellness approach called Mindfulness, which is respecting your body enough to give it the power to get better on itself. That was personal integrity and from it came the need to help others achieve wellness and what I learnt on my wellness journey shaped my professional integrity.

Integrity shapes and promotes a positive working environment where employees produce high-quality work despite uncertainties and the client's needs are fully met. Here, employees feel seen and appreciated not just for their efforts. Communication is fully present as the leader leads by being open to even difficult conversations. Overall, the working teams are inspired to be productive and resilient holding strong values such as patience, flexibility, responsibility for one's mistakes, and commitment. Moreover, leaders with integrity set up boundaries thus showing respect for others and themselves while fervently pouring into their work as if they do while attending their juniors. Integrity is being true and sincere in your service to others and yourself. Integrity is standing firm in your values even when no one is looking.

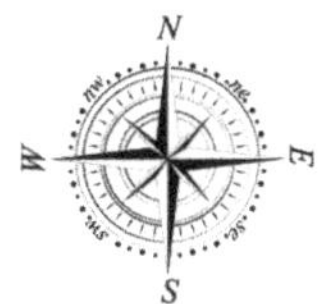

Muriel Blanc on Integrity

Leadership and Integrity: Navigating the Inner Compass

In the quiet sanctuary of transformational coaching, a journey of profound introspection unfolds. A canvas painted with threads of intuition and healing energy, where the artistry of leadership and integrity intertwine, forming a tapestry of empowerment and growth. As we embark upon this voyage of self-discovery, let us engage not only the mind but also the senses that guide us through the realm of experience.

Sight: The Illumination of Integrity Imagine stepping into a realm where the ethereal glow of authenticity casts an iridescent light upon every thought and action. In the realm of leadership, integrity stands as the beacon, a lighthouse that guides our choices and decisions. Just as an artist meticulously chooses each color to create a masterpiece, a true leader selects the hues of honesty, transparency, and accountability. In the tapestry of moral compass, integrity is the thread that weaves each strand of interaction into a harmonious symphony.

Touch: The Texture of Connection Leadership without touch is like a canvas devoid of texture – it lacks depth and resonance. A transformational leader possesses the ability to reach beyond the surface, to feel the pulse of their

Team's emotions, fears, and aspirations. Just as an intuitive artist senses the pulse of a brushstroke, the leader's touch evokes empathy, connection, and a profound understanding of the human experience. The power of touch, both literal and metaphorical, ignites trust and nurtures collaboration, creating an environment where growth flourishes like a vibrant garden.

Taste: The Essence of Authenticity

Leadership, when imbued with integrity, becomes an elegant blend of flavors that tantalize the palate of trust. Just as connoisseurs savor the layers of fine wine, an intuitive leader relishes in the authenticity of their actions. The taste of integrity is both subtle and bold, leaving a lasting impression that lingers like the aftertaste of a memorable meal. An authentic leader understands that their actions, words, and intentions are the ingredients that infuse the team's journey with meaning and purpose.

Hearing: The Symphony of Communication

The artistry of leadership resonates through the symphony of communication, where words are notes and actions are melodies. Like an intuitive artist attuned to the harmony of colors, a transformational leader listens not only to what is spoken but also to the unspoken emotions beneath. The cadence of honesty and compassion creates a resonance that transcends mere conversation, reaching the depths of understanding. Through the act of listening, a leader weaves threads of connection that bind the team together, forging a powerful alliance of shared purpose.

Smell: The Aroma of Inspiration

The fragrance of integrity, like a delicate bouquet, permeates the atmosphere of leadership. Just as an intuitive artist is invigorated by the scents of nature, a transformational leader draws inspiration from the essence of their values. The scent of integrity infuses every interaction, leaving an indelible impression upon the senses of all who cross its path. It sparks a desire for growth, awakens dormant potentials, and creates an environment where innovation flourishes like wildflowers in a sunlit meadow.

In the grand tapestry of leadership and integrity, these senses intertwine, creating a masterpiece that goes beyond the canvas of the ordinary. As we step into the realm of transformational coaching and intuitive leadership, we must remember that our moral compass guides us not merely through the rough seas of decision-making, but into the heart of authenticity, empathy, and empowerment.

Just as a skilled artist blends hues to evoke emotions, a leader blends integrity, authenticity, and empathy to evoke transformation. By engaging all five senses, we can cultivate an environment where leadership becomes a work of art, an ever-evolving creation that reflects the beauty of the human spirit.

In this symphony of senses, let us embrace the profound journey of leadership and integrity, painting a legacy that transcends time – a legacy of empowerment, growth, and the unwavering commitment to navigate by the true north of our moral compass.

Parisa Rose on Integrity

Integrity: The Ultimate Compass

Within the layers of life, where numerous variables converge and inter-play, certain principles remain constant. Among these constants, there exists a principle so profound that its significance and impact cannot be understated. Its greatest strength is found in personal embodiment rather than acquisition, and that principle is integrity.

Integrity, in its essence, is about truth. It is about saying the truth, acting out the truth, and embodying the truth. As a leader, remember you are always a leader of your own life; you are entrusted with the stewardship of others' experiences that accumulate into their futures. This responsibility necessitates that you be radically truthful, first to yourself, then to those in your sphere of influence and those who follow you. When you act with integrity, you become a beacon in the chaos, a point of reference that others can rely upon.

Much like the archetypal hero journeying through the underworld to slay the dragon of chaos, a leader with integrity ventures into the complex landscapes of organizational dynamics, economic uncertainty, and human nature. The integrity they carry is their sword, their shield, and their compass, guiding them in the face of the unknown and arming them against the obstacles they encounter.

We must also understand that integrity is not merely about being honest when it is convenient, but it is about standing for the truth when it is inconvenient or challenging. It is found in our actions when no one is around to account for our micro decisions. It is about being truthful even when the deceit appears to offer an easier path. Being a commitment to integrity shows a willingness to hold a boundary for the sake of protecting values and the bigger picture. This is the crucible in which fortitude and trust are forged.

The lack of integrity, however, can be likened to a ship without a rudder. Such a ship might be fine in calm seas but let a storm arise, and it becomes directionless, unable to navigate the tumultuous waters. It is a ship that is prone to capsizing. So is the human and leader without integrity.

Integrity is an inside job but a collective responsibility so we get to delve into our own psyche first in order to discover the recipe of meeting people where they are. We get to explore the implications of integrating or failing to integrate this core principle into our own life practice. We get to draw from clinical psychology, curiosity, and lived experiences to start building a comprehensive understanding of why integrity is not just a moral choice, but also an existential necessity for anyone aspiring to lead a life of meaningful impact.

Remember, you cannot lead others where you are not willing to go yourself. To ask others to operate with integrity, you must first do so yourself. Therefore, leading with integrity always starts on the inside and radiates outward. It starts with you, and what an honor that is. After all, the first step in setting the world straight is to make sure our own house is in order. And the cornerstone of that order is integrity.

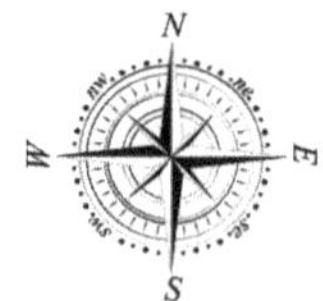

Pattie Godfrey~Sadler on Integrity

"Honesty is the Best Policy"

Integrity is a concept that is probably the most important of traits. Although we use it to describe a person's character, it is so much more than that.

Integrity is a way of living that is based on values and principles that guide a person's behavior. It is a way of living that is honest, responsible, and respectful of others. It cannot be faked or forced, as it is a way of being.

Growing up I learned many lessons of integrity from my father, Kenneth Godfrey. He was a bank manager for many years and was truly a people person. During his life, he was exemplary in all his actions from day to day. He was trustworthy, honest, patient, kind, unconditionally loving, and had a larger-than-life Faith in God. He was a testament to me in my lifetime of the most important trait a person can ever have, honesty. He always said, "Honesty is the best policy."

Throughout my life, I have used this mantra even at difficult times when I did not necessarily want to share the truth. It has been a very strong characteristic that I developed throughout my life from his fine example. Being honest about situations in my life, in my opinions, and my responses when speaking with others has been probably the easiest task for me.

Sometimes the truth hurts, but I would rather hurt you with the truth so you can trust my word rather than wonder about my motives. I have none. No motives. Integrity is a process of learning to be honest and accountable for our actions. Being true to oneself and to others is the most important of traits.

Having a strong sense of self-worth and self-respect is paramount to having integrity. Look, if I could give any advice to my grandchildren, or my kids, it would be the same that my father gave me years ago.

Honesty is the best policy. Always. No exceptions.

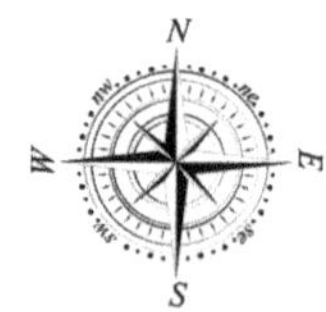

Rex Sikes on Integrity

Don't Just Be an Empty Suit.
Be a Person of Integrity.

"Perhaps the most crucial choice we make in life is who to trust."

– Stewart Stafford

Too many people who dress for success seek to impress others with what they wear and what they own. Better to impress people by <u>who</u> you are than by possessions. Better to be genuine, than a façade.

What the world needs more than ever are compassionate, honest leaders with true integrity, committed to creating excellence through harmony. Living breathing examples of walking the talk, not people just dressed up. Do not be an empty suit. You can either look impressive or BE impressive. Here is how.

You may lack riches, a car, or even a home, but there is one thing you have. Your word. *Your word is your bond.* People of integrity keep their word.

When you break your promises, your commitments, your appointments, you shout, "I don't care." You lack integrity; you are not someone worth knowing. Do not take your words lightly. Others want to trust them. If they cannot, they cannot trust you.

Trust is earned. Once broken it is difficult, it may be impossible, to get it back. Do not lose it. What you say and do broadcasts your values. Whether that is spending most of your energy in pursuit of money, fame, power, family, justice, or community. Do you seek to serve, or do you seek to take? Others can tell.

Seek to go the extra mile and serve others first. Seek to uplift, support, and edify. Treat others like gold and they are more apt to value and support you.

True leaders do not call themselves leaders because they need to impress. They are focused on the message, <u>not</u> the messenger. A tour bus driver does not talk about his amazing driving skills; he helps travelers explore a new world. Focus on the listener and the goal you are working toward together.

Act to empower others, not to take credit for it.

When Jesus healed, he did not say, "Look what I just did." He said, "*Your* faith has made *you* whole."

True leaders give credit to those they lead, yet when things do not work out, leaders take responsibility. Leaders do not blame.

If there are problems communicating, they make amends. They adjust to feedback because they are open to constructive positive criticism.

Leading is easier and more effective when the interests of others are first in your heart. Listen and be responsive. Act with love and respect. Inspire by example. Those who realize you genuinely care, value your guidance. They are willing to follow your lead because they can trust you.

Empowering others is not a sign of weakness. You must be secure in yourself to hold others in your heart.

Broken individuals do not make good leaders. To help people become their best, leaders do not insist others change first. They start with themselves.

To be a good leader you must first be a good follower. To be a good teacher you must first be a good student. Be open to seeking wise console from those smarter and wiser than you seek.

Ultimately, the great leader is willing to do whatever he asks of others, as well as willing to do what others are not. The leader *wants* others to surpass him or her.

It is not about being a 'top dog' but about helping others reach the top.

Power comes from love, kindness, patience, understanding, and giving. You do not have to grab and hold onto power when you serve others well. When you add so much value to those you serve, they will want you to remain in place.

Seek to heal, not to criticize. Seek to unite not to divide. The person of integrity does what is necessary to repair the relationship. They become more attentive and more respectful, they listen *more*, without judgment to understand.

You will know you are a leader when you always act with integrity, walk your talk, and are honest and trustworthy. When all is said and done, YOU only have yourself. You came in with nothing and will go out the same. Not even the fancy suit

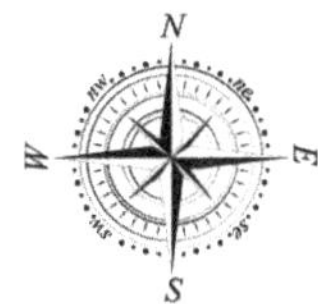

Rita Montalto on Integrity

ntegrity is a super vital trait for a leader. It encompasses honesty, transparency, accountability, and reliability.

It is the foundation of trust and credibility that leaders must build with their team, customers, and partners.

In today's world, where ethics and morality are often questioned, leaders must prioritize integrity to create a better world not just for themselves but the world around them.

Integrity can achieve more when combined with one important trait: emotional intelligence. Emotional intelligence is the ability to recognize and understand one's emotions and those of others. This trait helps leaders empathize with their team members, understand their perspectives, and create a culture of collaboration, innovation, and empathy.

When leaders with high emotional intelligence come together, they can create a culture that fosters a sense of belonging, trust, and commitment.

If I had to give you an example then ….I cannot help but think of the futuristic show Star Trek and its captains, talk about emotional intelligence and integrity on steroids!

As an optimist, I believe that emotional intelligence and integrity will make a significant impact on the world and how humanity lives. When we prioritize these traits in all aspects of our lives, we create a ripple effect of positive change that can extend far beyond our immediate circle of influence.

However, how can we raise future leaders who possess the ability to uphold integrity and practice emotional intelligence? In the book 'Think and Grow Rich,' Napoleon Hill emphasizes the importance of personal development in achieving success.

I have made it my mission to prioritize personal development in a fun and engaging way through a digital game and that is exactly what I am creating as my contribution to raising our future generation of leaders.

From the moment, those pages of 'Think and Grow Rich' touched my hands; a flame was ignited within me. It was as if the words on the page were speaking directly to my soul, urging me to push past my limits and reach for greatness. I remember those late nights, poring over the pages; my eyes heavy with fatigue, but my mind alight with possibility.

Moreover, from that moment on, I was consumed by a hunger for knowledge and growth. I devoured every possible personal development book, course, and seminar that crossed my path, investing in my education with a fervor that some might call crazy. However, to me, it was all worth it, because I knew that the knowledge I was gaining was leading me down a path of success and fulfillment and helping others to rise.

I spent over two decades as a hairdresser, a career that I loved dearly. Nevertheless, as I found myself spending more time talking to my clients about their mindset and personal growth than their hair, I knew that it was time for a change. Therefore, I took the leap, transitioning to this beautiful, exciting new world of personal development.

The journey has not always been easy, but every step has been worth it. Because now, I am living a life of purpose and passion, helping others to unlock their full potential and reach for their dreams. In addition, it all started with words on a page that sparked a fire within me that will never be extinguished.

Now on the second of three phases of my project, the 4-Pillars of Wealth: The Success Game is a digital game derived from the teachings of Napoleon Hill and other thought leaders that focuses on developing emotional, spiritual, physical, and monetary wealth. My dream is to have this personal development game in high schools and in workplaces to inspire and empower the next generation to prioritize emotional intelligence and integrity in their lives.

By playing the game, individuals can learn about themselves, their values, and their goals. They can develop emotional intelligence, enhance their spirituality, improve their physical health, learn about financial management, and strengthen both values and skills that empower them to lead a life of integrity and emotional intelligence.

Leaders must be willing to confront their weaknesses, acknowledge their mistakes, and take responsibility for their actions. They must be willing to make tough decisions that align with their values, even if it means going against the norm. Leadership requires self-awareness, self-reflection, and a willingness to learn and grow continuously. Imagine having the ability to learn and practice these skills and traits through a digital game. It is time to raise a new breed of leaders.

Leaders who prioritize personal development and possess high emotional intelligence and integrity can create a ripple effect of positive change. When we prioritize emotional intelligence and integrity on a societal level, we can create a world that is more just, equitable, enjoyable, and sustainable. I look forward to playing Four Pillars of wealth with you someday.

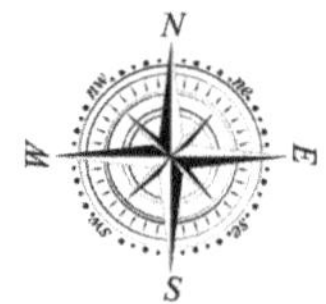

Ryan Matsumore on Integrity

It is 5:05 am, and I wake and experience the middle state of not being able to sleep while also resisting getting up. I am also aware I have the opportunity to share on the topic of "Integrity" and decide to go to the living room in the house I am visiting in Cuernavaca, Mexico.

It is still dark and I chose to sit with my favorite Joe Dispenza meditation. As I press play I set the intention for "What does the world need to know about integrity?" The response that arises is "What do I need to know about integrity?" as I am one microcosm of the whole. The only way for me to know what "the world needs to know about integrity" will come from looking inside and admitting what it is I need to know about integrity...

Maybe integrity isn't a thing, maybe it is a process? Could integrity be personified by honoring my experience that we are all a microcosm of the whole and sharing that here with you now? Maybe to be in integrity all we get to do is look within, discern our gifts and distortions, and express them honestly to others and ourselves.

Might integrity be owning and admitting that the only way we can change the world is by changing ourselves? The only way to overcome the complex challenges of the world is to overcome the complex challenges inside ourselves. Maybe if we each chose to live this way, we would each be and become exactly what is needed in each new moment and circumstance life brings.

The alternative I see is the one we live in now where we are pointing fingers at others and saying "This person, that person, and those people need to change." This approach only creates a world where everyone is pointing fingers while nothing actually changes.

Maybe integrity is responsibility. Responsibility meaning - being honest with myself and focusing 100% of my energy on changing the 1% I am wrong. When I say "wrong" I do not mean a binary yes/no or good/bad context, I mean - that which is not aligned with healthy love.

Might my expression here be an embodiment or fragrance integrity? Is integrity admitting I do not know what integrity "is" I only know what it means to me in each moment as I choose to embody and express it authentically?

All I know is that this is a written documentation of my morning and me, to be received, tasted or digested by you, if you choose. This is my truth in this moment and one that continues to consistently arise. Does its consistent message over and over point to an absolute truth or am I wise enough to know that it is only my ego that's excited by ideas of absolute truths? I choose the latter and give full space for your truths. You and I are microcosms of the whole.

At this moment, this expression feels complete for me and I am also aware of a 900 word count available for this share. So for those who want more, here is more:

Here are a series of questions that will support you if you choose to let them. The full expression of this choice would be taking the time to get out a sheet of paper and write down your responses while allowing yourself the space to elaborate on each as far and as deep as it feels important.

—-- A PRACTICAL INTEGRITY PRACTICE —--

YOUR PAST:

1. What have you been taught "integrity" is?
2. Who taught you this?
3. What are examples of how these meanings about integrity have supported you?
4. What are examples of how these meanings about integrity have held you back?
5. What are you learning now about integrity?

e.g., I was taught integrity was giving everything you have and keeping your word no matter what. I was taught (I interpreted this as a child) this by my Dad and Mom. How it supported me was being able to trust myself to follow through and others to trust me as reliable. How this "rule" held me back was that I stayed in romantic relationships longer than I should have. With this mindset, I had to give it my all and "make" it work no matter what, all while missing that the relationship was not truly aligned. I learned that maybe my original definition of integrity was….incomplete.

RIGHT NOW:

1. What does integrity mean to you right now?
2. How is this supporting you right now?
3. How is this holding you back right now?
4. How is this supporting your family, community, and the world in its entirety?
5. How is this incomplete and holding back your family, community, and the world in its entirety?
6. What are you learning about integrity?

EACH NEW NOW OF YOUR LIFE:

1. What best serves you? (knowing that what best serves you is what also best serves all others)
2. Does it serve you to have a definition of "integrity"?
3. Does it serve you to instead have an evolving story of integrity you are aware of each day and express authentically?
4. What is integrity for you?

—-- PRACTICE COMPLETE —--

Webster's Definition of Integrity:

1. As in morality:
    a. Conduct that conforms to an accepted standard of right and wrong

2. As in honesty:

Devotion to telling the truth

3. As in honor:

Faithfulness to high moral standards

Ryan Tomoharu Matsumori's Essence of Integrity:

1. Today - all above!

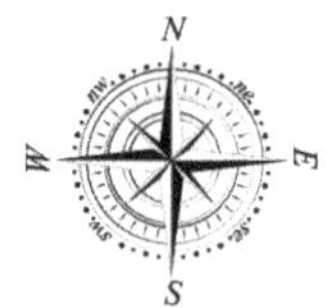

Sandra Horton on Integrity

Pathways to Identify Your Integrity in Business

Hi, my name is Sandra J. Horton. I serve as a Business Success Coach. My focus is on Change Management. I help people create paths of change in business and in leadership. As a Business Success Coach, I start to identify the business its purpose, systems, and strategies. I focus on the essence of the company by breaking down the identity "reputation" (purpose, value, and mission) but the most interesting is the truth of the company – its integrity.

Integrity for business is best described as a pathway between the business/owner, workers/leadership, with the client journey including products and services. Integrity is the truth in that each part must uphold. If one of these is out of balance, then as a whole it suffers. By knowing your integrity as a business, you will be able to see the pathways using certain tips, tools, and insights to navigate your way through change. Accepting and implementing change requires knowing what your business stands for in all aspects. The wholeness creates the identity of the company.

In business, I focus on the integrity of the company's six levels.

The first level is Accountability, which is to have clear and open communication across all levels of the organization.

The second level is to have Responsibility, which is about taking radical leadership for all aspects of your business.

The third level is Ethics where we see the moral principal foundation of the company and its people.

The fourth is Commitment where there is dedication to the vision of the company, as a whole.

The fifth is ensuring Sustainability, which will ensure a positive impact for future generations.

The sixth level is Innovation where a company is open for improvements, change, and growth.

When I evaluate these six levels of integrity, I will quickly see the gaps, hidden issues, and inefficiencies within an organization. Applying Conscious Leadership Strategies, Change Management and Emotional Intelligence will unlock the pathways to activate success.

Strategies for leaders to live in integrity are best illustrated by being trustworthy, authentic, responsible, grateful, curious, self-lead, and open to learning.

Individual integrity is paramount to being a conscious leader in today's business environment. By identifying, your integrity will allow you to feel fulfilled and empowered. Integrity is the truth of your reputation that precedes you. My invitation as a Business Success Coach is to get to understand yourself intimately by building self-awareness. Integrity is the key to living a successful life.

Positive strategies for honoring your integrity and building rapport:

- Be intentional and be in Action: communicate clearly about what you want to do and follow through.
- Respond not react: Take a deep breath and seek to understand what is showing up.
- Positive Mindset: Be open to learning through at any moment the opportunities and possibilities that are present.
- Open communication: Acknowledge that everyone goes through change at his or her own pace.
- Be Conscious: Be present, stay in the now.

In closing, integrity is the cornerstone of great leadership. Choose to learn, live, and lead (3L's) as a Conscious leader in your life and business now.

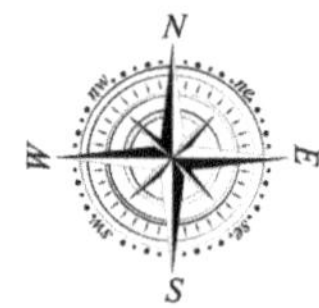

Sandee Sgarlata on Integrity

When I contemplate the essence of integrity, in my opinion, it revolves around being in integrity with yourself. Being in integrity with yourself is a profound concept, encompassing various aspects of personal honesty, ethical conduct, and authenticity. It involves living in a manner that is consistent with your values, beliefs, and principles, ensuring that your actions align with your inner moral compass. This internal consistency is at the heart of self-respect and self-trust, forming the foundation upon which you build your interactions with the world.

The journey toward personal integrity begins with self-awareness. It requires an introspective look into your own values, beliefs, and motivations. Understanding what truly matters to you is pivotal in setting a course that is in harmony with your inner self. It means having the courage to stand apart from the crowd when necessary and to uphold your beliefs even in the face of opposition.

Being in integrity also means being honest with yourself. It involves acknowledging your flaws and weaknesses as areas for growth and improvement. This self-honesty fosters a sense of humility, keeping you connected to the reality of being perfectly human.

Consistency with your actions is another critical aspect of being in integrity. This consistency is not about rigidity or inflexibility, but rather about maintaining a clear moral and ethical direction even when it's challenging. It means making choices that are not always easy or popular but are in line with your principles. This could manifest in small daily decisions or significant life choices, each equally important in maintaining personal integrity.

Integrity also involves responsibility and accountability. It means owning up to your mistakes and learning from them, rather than deflecting blame or making excuses. This level of accountability not only promotes personal growth but also builds trust and respect in your relationships with others. When you are in integrity, people around you know that you are reliable and that your word holds weight.

Moreover, living in integrity has a profound impact on your mental and emotional well-being. It brings a sense of peace and contentment, knowing that you are living a life true to yourself. It reduces internal conflict, which may arise when there is a mismatch between your actions and your values. This inner harmony is crucial for long-term happiness and fulfillment. Lastly, being in integrity with yourself sets a powerful example for others. It inspires and encourages those around you to also seek authenticity and honesty in their lives. In a world where superficiality and inauthenticity are rampant, choosing to live with integrity is a bold and impactful statement. It creates a ripple effect, influencing your community and, potentially, society at large.

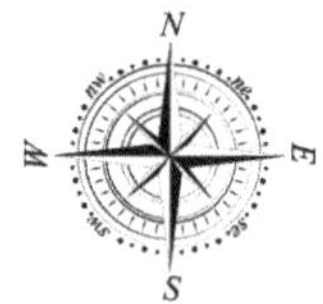

Sherry Gideons on Integrity

As I reflect on the past 27 years of my life's journey, I am reminded of the profound transformation I have undergone—a journey marked by self-discovery and mastery over the concept of integrity. This chapter is not just an attempt to share the lessons I have learned along the way, but a heartfelt invitation to explore the depths of my understanding, shaped by the trials and triumphs of life.

Chasing an Elusive Ideal:

My first near-death experience was a result of my immersion in the professional bodybuilding and fitness industry. It was a time when societal perspectives on the "perfect" female body were evolving rapidly. The pressure to conform to industry standards and meet the ever-shifting expectations was overwhelming. In my pursuit of that elusive ideal, I found myself at a crossroads.

During this experience, I had an awakening. As my life hung in the balance, I realized that integrity was not just about adhering to external standards—it was about staying true to my inner values. It meant rejecting the temptation of shortcuts and embracing a path of authenticity. This moment set the stage for my ongoing journey towards understanding the guiding principle of integrity.

The Painful Path to Self-Discovery

Over the years, life presented me with numerous challenges, both personal and professional. The pain, suffering, and setbacks became my greatest teachers. Through it all, integrity emerged as a beacon of light guiding me through the darkest of times. It meant maintaining moral consistency in the face of adversity and choosing the path of honesty and authenticity, even when it seemed difficult.

The Second NDE: A Spiritual Awakening

My second near-death experience came after years of working with universal laws and learning from some of the greatest spiritual teachers. During this time, one of my twins was born with extraordinary challenges—no throat, half vertebrae's, a hole in her heart, and double hernias. It was a time of immense personal and emotional growth.

After delivering my twins, I experienced a massive heart attack in which I was told I would die without a heart transplant. Yet, through the principles of affirmative prayer, I managed to heal from just 37 percent heart function to a state of 100% wholeness. Today, my 19-year-old daughter, whom you would never know had any health issues, stands as a testament to the power of spiritual growth and healing.

Discovering Your Moral Compass

But this journey isn't just about my own experiences and how I discovered the tools that continually kept me aligned with my own intentional integrity, but also about how others can discover their own moral compass. It begins with clarity and awareness of whom you truly choose to be in life. It means taking the time to understand your core values and what matters most to you.

Being present in the moment is another essential aspect of this journey. It is not an idealistic approach, and far from reach. It is about recognizing that each moment is an opportunity to align your actions with your moral compass. It is a commitment to living with intention and mindfulness, making choices that reflect your true self.

Furthermore, it is about having the willingness and desire to be a light of infinite possibility for others. Integrity is not a solitary pursuit; it is a way of being that ripples out to touch the lives of those around you. It means being a source of inspiration, guidance, transformation, and support for others on their own journeys of self-discovery and integrity.

Through 27 years of self-discovery, spiritual growth, and life mastery, I have learned that integrity is not static. It is not merely a word or a concept but a living, breathing principle that guides our actions and choices. It is about being true to ourselves and our inner values, even in the face of external pressures or shifting expectations.

Integrity is a reflection of our character, and it is a testament to our strength as human beings. It means practicing what we preach and aligning our actions with our moral compass, no matter the challenges we encounter on our journey.

Here are some actionable steps you can use on your own journey of Self Mastery

1. Self-Reflection: Begin by taking time for self-reflection. Consider your life's journey and the choices you have made. Think about the moments when you felt most true to yourself and when you deviated from your core values.

2. Identify Core Values: Take an inventory of your core values. What principles guide your life? List them out and prioritize them. Understand what truly matters to you.

3. Clarity and Awareness: Gain clarity about who you truly want to be in life. Ask yourself what kind of person you aspire to become. Cultivate self-awareness to recognize when you are in alignment with your values and when you are not.

4. Mindfulness Practice: Practice being present in the moment. Mindfulness helps you make conscious choices that align with your moral compass. Start with short daily exercises to cultivate this habit.

5. Commit to Authenticity: Make a commitment to living authentically. This means being true to your core values and acting in alignment with them, even when it is challenging or uncomfortable.

6. Learn from Setbacks: Embrace setbacks and failures as opportunities for growth. Instead of viewing them negatively, see them as lessons

that can strengthen your integrity. Take responsibility for your actions and learn from your mistakes.

7. Seek Guidance: Seek guidance from mentors, spiritual teachers, or individuals who embody the kind of integrity you aspire to. Learning from others can provide valuable insights and support.

8. Practice Affirmative Prayer: If applicable, explore the principles of affirmative prayer or other spiritual practices that resonate with you. These practices can help you tap into your inner strength and potential for healing and growth.

9. Be a Source of Inspiration: Extend your journey of integrity by becoming a source of inspiration and support for others. Share your experiences and insights with those who may benefit from your wisdom.

10. Stay Open to Growth: Recognize that integrity is a lifelong journey. Stay open to personal growth and be willing to adapt as your understanding of yourself and your values evolves.

11. Trust the Inner Source: Develop trust in the inner source within you. Have faith that it can guide you towards a life of greater integrity, purpose, and meaning.

As I reflect on my journey, I can say that the path has been arduous at times, but it has also been illuminating. Through every twist and turn, I have discovered the true essence of integrity—a guiding force that has led me toward a life defined by authenticity, honesty, and unwavering moral consistency. A trust and a faith in allowing the source within me to reveal the many avenues, channels, and ways for me to be a continual vessel to demonstrate good and greater good that is available to us all when we remain true to our integrity. It is a journey I would not trade for anything, for it has illuminated the path to a life of profound integrity and purpose, and I hope it can do the same for you.

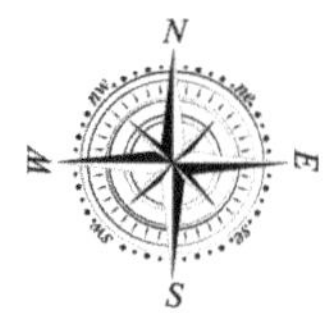

Yasmine Saad on Integrity

The Essence of Integrity-Driven Leadership

As a psychologist leading an award-winning group practice, I follow ten essential principles for leading with integrity.

1. "Lead through your presence: integrity flows from within"

    How does your presence reflect the standards you set? The values you promote come from "who you are" rather than your desired outcomes. They are not merely intellectual morals but genuine reflections of your character. You are the foundation of trust and respect among your team members, so instead of setting expectations, embody them. It will set the tone for your team to adhere to them.

2. "Cultivate compassion to nurture integrity."

    What does it mean to lead with compassion? By prioritizing empathy and understanding, you can create deeper connections with your employees, fostering a sense of respect, and genuine appreciation leading to motivation to work towards shared goals.

3. "Seek the potential within."

    How can bringing out the best in others be an integrity driven approach to leadership? When you focus on nurturing inherent qualities that already exist within each team member, you show your respect and align their individual values with the organization. This fosters a work culture rooted in authenticity.

4. "Embrace self-awareness to ensure authenticity.»

    Why is self-awareness important in integrity-driven leadership? Through self-awareness, you can embrace all aspects of yourself and honestly lead. This promotes a more open and transparent work environment.

5. "Nurture curiosity to transcend judgment."

   What does curiosity promote integrity? Curiosity liberates you from judgment, fostering understanding and more effective feedback.

6. "Strengthen trust to fortify integrity; build it through honesty, fairness, and commitment."

   How can we foster trust for integrity-driven leadership? By consistently demonstrating honesty, fairness, and commitment, you will create a trusting work environment. Moreover, by working on trusting yourself, you will lead with integrity.

7. "Fortify your courage to speak your truth and embrace feedback."

   What does it take to maintain integrity while providing or hearing feedback? Develop the confidence to address conflicts constructively, fostering a culture of open communication within your team so that integrity can be maintained.

8. "Embrace humility for your ongoing growth journey."

   How can integrity be rooted in humility? Humility promotes honesty and honesty leads to integrity. This creates a culture of continuous learning and growth, fostering a sense of ongoing improvement among your team members.

9. "Align your words and actions."

   Why is coherence between preaching and practicing crucial? Coherence between actions and words strengthens trust and respect and builds integrity.

10. "Practice consistency."

   How does consistency reinforce integrity? Striving for consistency in your leadership approach will further strengthen your team's trust and respect.

By incorporating these guiding principles, you foster an environment rooted in integrity and authenticity. This enhances team relationships and organizational success and enhances individual and collective achievements. This approach cultivates trust and respect, leading to genuine, effective leadership that can be applied to all fields.

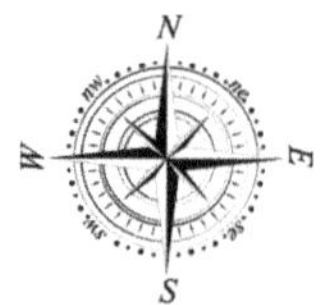

Yve Ruiz on Integrity

Living anchored in Integrity

When we think of someone who is not in integrity, images of a bully, a cheating spouse, or an embezzler may arise. Someone who prioritizes their exploitive agenda over respecting another's needs.

It might never occur to us that not being in integrity can look like Morgan, the moral church lady who feeds the homeless, has never gotten a speeding ticket, and offers freely a comforting shoulder to lean on. She may appear to be the epitome of integrity.

Well, let us look more closely. While Morgan smiles and laughs with friends, her smile fades and she becomes more pensive at home with her husband Rick. Before Morgan married him, she loved working and was offered a promotion. Then fiancé Rick told her she did not need to work anymore. He told everyone at church that it was because he wanted to take care of her like a princess.

Although over the years since marrying, she has expressed to him an interest in going back to work, he has held his ground. Recently, he began blaming her for overspending, when in fact, Morgan keeps impeccable track of her expenditures and they remain consistent.

Now, many of us tend to think about integrity as an agreement between two or more people to mutually express respect, openly and honestly communicate, and keep promises. This is interpersonal integrity. When it is present, transactions among people go smoothly.

Often forgotten is intrapersonal integrity. We all have running mental conversations of our own. We ask ourselves questions and usually answer back. Our commentary can be supportive, honest, and respectful to ourselves or it can be dismissive, dishonest, and disrespectful.

Morgan happened to marry someone who intentionally charmed and reeled her in, only to devalue her over time while making demands and manipulating her for his satisfaction. She is in a narcissistic relationship.

Morgan considers herself completely as integral. Her compassionate heart sings when she serves and supports others. However, deep down, Morgan knows she deserves more respect, caring, and empathy from Rick. However, he blames her for his behavior. She mentally replays Rick's ongoing negative critique of her. Then while focusing more on pleasing him, Morgan neglects herself.

One day, Amanda, her best friend, takes her out for lunch and reflects on how Morgan is treating herself. It is as if Morgan is consistently ignoring a heartbroken friend who approaches her for comfort and support. Despite her caring for everyone else in real life, Morgan lacks integrity – toward herself.

Morgan sits in disbelief. She does not have it in her heart to dismiss a friend suffering beside her. How could Morgan have turned her back on herself? For years? Morgan realizes she has gotten so used to being overlooked at home that it has come to feel natural.

Morgan's insight sparks a profound inner shift. With newfound clarity, she starts small yet impactful changes in her life. Introspection and self-reflection become Morgan's morning sanctuary, allowing her to explore authentic self-assessment, emotions, and desires without Rick's judgment.

Morgan enlists the aid of an expert who specializes in helping people recognize, recover from, and rebuild their lives after narcissistic relationships. Because of their educational and experiential sessions, Morgan gains self-compassion and learns how to navigate Rick's manipulative tactics, enforce healthy boundaries, and assert her needs.

Over time, Morgan's self-respect and resilience bloom. As she steps more fully into her integrity, Morgan develops a newfound sense of empowerment and inner strength. She returns to work and eventually is promoted. Morgan shares her success story when offering support to others who find themselves in similar situations.

Morgan's journey serves as a testament to the transformative power of using healthy social and professional support to reclaim one's intrapersonal integrity in a narcissistic relationship. She chooses integrity daily, knowing it is not a one-time event but an ongoing commitment to honor herself and cultivate authentic relationships built on trust and mutual respect.

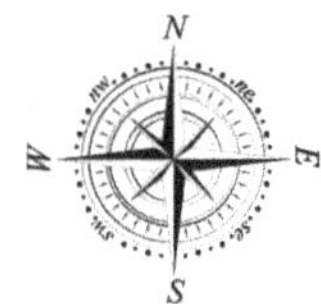

Closing Remarks: The Journey Beyond-Embracing Your Moral Compass

As we draw the curtains on this book and reflect on the journey, we have undertaken together, it is important to recognize that the true essence of our exploration begins now, as the last page turns. The world awaits you, a canvas ready for the brushstrokes of your integrity and the guidance of your inner moral compass, leading you toward becoming the best version of yourself.

Throughout these pages, we have navigated the intricate landscapes of moral and ethical decision-making, delving deep into what it means to live with integrity. Remember, the value of these lessons is not confined to the realm of theory or discussion. Their true worth emerges as you apply them in the diverse scenarios of your daily life.

Integrity is more than a concept; it is a living, breathing practice. It is present in the small, seemingly insignificant choices you make every day. It is in the way you respond to challenges, how you handle success and setbacks, and the authenticity of your interactions with others.

As you step forward from this point, let your moral compass be your guide. This compass is not just a tool for navigating through dilemmas; it is a beacon that illuminates your path, helping you stay true to your values and principles. It is about being consistent in your actions, aligning your deeds with your deepest beliefs, and being the same person in public as you are in private.

The journey of integrity is ongoing and ever evolving. Each day presents new opportunities to learn, grow, and influence the world around you positively.

Embrace these opportunities, for in them lies the potential to not only transform your life but also to inspire those around you.

As you move forward, remember that your actions, driven by integrity, have the power to impact and inspire. The way you live your life, the decisions you make, and the way you lead can set a precedent, encouraging others to follow in the path of honesty, respect, and ethical behavior.

In closing, I encourage you to take everything you have learned and apply it with courage and conviction. Let your moral compass be your steadfast guide as you navigate the complexities of life. Your journey does not end here; it takes on a new dimension, enriched by the wisdom and understanding you have gained.

Thank you for embarking on this journey with me. May the path ahead be guided by the unwavering light of your moral compass, leading you to a life filled with purpose, integrity, and genuine fulfillment!